Between Two Doors

and other short stories

BY

PATTI DORSEY-GUMP

Copyright © 2014
All rights reserved. No part of this book may be reproduced, stored, or transmitted by any means—whether auditory, graphic, mechanical, or electronic—without the written permission of both publisher and author, except in the case of brief excerpts used in critical articles and reviews. Unauthorized reproduction of any part of this work is illegal and is punishable by law.

ISBN-10: 1494469197
ISBN-13: 978-1494469191

DEDICATION

I would like to first dedicate this book to the journey that God has given us, whether we like it or not.

To my brother, Terry Dorsey who was there for a lifetime, holding me up when things got tough and still put a smile on my face.

Thank you to all my lifetime friends who were always there for me....Beth Bohmer, Tricia Goodlett, Judy Riley, Judy Bulmer, June Rising, Barb Ferris and Dr. Jane Gardner.

To my lifelong best friend, Amy Aldworth-Steiner, my rock who understood everything and made sure we both laughed hilariously about it.

But this book is mostly for my son who would have liked to lock me away many times because of my silliness and unusual way of viewing the world. Without him this book would not have come to fruition. He is my life and my joy and when everyone else had died, he was the reason I didn't. Thank you, my Sweetheart.

Contents

Title	Page
Between Two Doors	1
In Irish Hopes	44
Two Unlucky Days	67
The Funny Side of Inner-City	78
The Whistler	93
The New Mail Lady	95
My Blue Heron	98
Ed the Love Bird	100

Between Two Doors

The October sky began tuning and
polishing her autumn...
After the sun had weathered her summer...
Revealing her songs of passion...
Through the colors of her leaves.

Parma, Ohio

I went by the old house today. If I had closed my eyes and been led into the neighborhood by someone else I would have opened them and found the street to be like all the other streets in Cleveland. I would have commented, no doubt, how awful it was to have grown up in such a mundane place. And yet, it took me off guard as to how safe I felt. For a moment I was more comforted than I had been decades ago, right around the day we left.

The houses were weathered from years of Ohio winter tantrums, where Mother Nature, like a menopausal woman, couldn't figure out if she was hot, cold, or just pissed off. They were still as narrow as a lady's shoe box, strategically plotted out like colored squares on a Monopoly board. Shutters, painted in various shades of yellows matched the awnings hugging the windows. The lawns were no bigger than a postage stamp and were neatly trimmed and manicured. An old oak tree still devoured the front lawn, my front lawn. The tree, my tree, Annie Acorn had been chopped down and pruned more than once from what I could see by its perpetually growing roots circling itself from one side to another.

The lone tree stood fixed for years with a shade that danced its way up to kiss my bedroom window with shapes and shadows that peppered my young and innocent thoughts and dreams. There had not been another tree left standing on the whole street, ironically named Orchard Avenue. This blank devouring emptiness gave the avenue an eerie impression that the sky would never go away.

If it weren't for the sun room and breezeway added onto the back of the house, the woodwork would have still displayed its buttery hue that sank with the mellowness of twilight. It was a secret insult at first that the present owners had altered my childhood home by changing so many things until my thoughts distracted me further down the street as I slowly recaptured any memory I had left.

I could close my eyes and see the neighborhood filled with children close in age, and similar in stance, wearing the same tattered grass stained dungarees, rolled up above their bobby socks. The boys played softball in between the traffic. Franco was the brazen Italian boy who spoke in incomplete sentences and fancied himself to be kin to Elvis with his wavy jet-black hair, mounting a pout on his lips. Elliot, the freckle-faced Irish bloodhound-Dalmatian mix, pretended to be the wiser of the two, standing at the pitcher's mound puffing out his chest like a rump roast.

"Look at them hooters." Franco wallowed in our female presence before slamming the softball our way. Elliott was miffed while watching the girls on the sidelines.

"Keep your eye on the ball," Elliott would whistle hoping the piercing sound of his gaping buck teeth would travel down to home base. Home base was usually someone's soiled ball cap that mysteriously moved either closer to the home team or far from first base, depending who was at bat, Italian Franco, or Elliott, the Irish lad. Italy or Ireland. It didn't much matter who was cheating in the end because we all had to show up and confess our sins anyway to Father Dominic or Father Patrick, every Saturday at church. We would receive our penance, say three Hail Mary's, and hope that Grandma, who brought us there in the first place to confess, wasn't sitting at the edge of the pew pretending to say her rosary while leaning toward the confessional to listen to every word. We would then emerge cleansed in the eyes of God and Grandma May, hook our skinny arms into hers, be whacked on the back of our head for any future criminal acts on our walk home to the weekly, dry as sandpaper roast beef and lumpy mashed potatoes, only to return to the ball field we called Orchard Avenue just to cheat all over again.

Elliot, the Irish and much younger lad, not quite as hungry for attention as the older boys, tried to keep peace between the hormones of the Celtic brothers, while his own Dalmatian freckled brown spots melted right off his arms onto his elbows. Young as he was, he was not about to let the Italian boys trump him, move the home base cap to their liking, call the shots and win the girls attention.

Mr. Sloane's house was diagonal to home base. Mr. Sloane was the neighborhood curmudgeon who hated the outdoors, hated being near people, obviously hated kids and sure enough hated food, as he was as thin as an index card.

"Get that god-dang ball off my lawn!" Mr. Sloane appeared on his front porch every day after peering one rounded eyeball through the curtains when the ball landed in his shrubs. "I'll have your sorry asses thrown in jail." Mr. Sloane kept the ball from us if he got to it first.

"I'm calling the police, you little punks." And it might be a good thing he did, too. If the police weren't already busy with Mrs. Robertson's running her husband off every time they had a domestic brawl, or Mr. Jenkins, absent-mindedly walking his way into the traffic to buy his non-filter cigarettes that spewed out darts of tobacco each time he coughed the air out of his black lungs. Yes, the cops needed something really important to do and Mr. Sloane would've been just the thing, chasing baseballs off an old geezer's lawn, three times a day.

When I heard one day that Mr. Sloane had died I had only one question: Do we get our balls back?

Squeak, a name lovingly branded to the one who screeched when he inhaled, was the only kid who could spit a stream of saliva through his front teeth, mimicking the sound of a June bug crunching under foot and still convince us that this was sexually appealing.

It was the boys who shaped us with their gazes, their winks, their nods. Word on the street had it that the Italian boys had grown into the Mafia like their father. This would explain the mock kitchen in the front of their house and the functional kitchen they sought refuge in the basement.

But to me, they were just the boys who squished worms between their toes by the sewers after a rainstorm, or stole kisses from girls in the manholes where the bank was being built. It was the boys who raced us to the tinny ragtime tunes of the popsicle man for a lemon pop just before bedtime.

The working man's cemetery "Our Lady of Kielbasi" was four blocks from our street. No one in their right mind would have walked by it without first dashing to the other end, holding their breaths so as not to wake any sleeping soul that might grab us and pull us into the Polish underworld.

The elementary school stood only a breath from that. Its walls were still the antiquated gray bricks. The parking lot outlined with cautionary yellow stripes surrounded the playground filled with blissful screams. The windows in the building weren't as massive to me now. But the pillars held it up at the entrance way like they were holding up the heavens.

I was glad I had returned. A storm was brewing on the horizon and the thunder stole my daydreams and set me back to the present moment. I felt as if I could traverse in and out of my lifetime right now, understanding clearly that everything started here, that everything was meant to be and yet understanding nothing had any direction at all. I now understood that nothing was easy, that everything came at a price, that souls were not intertwined until a oneness is completed. But in this moment, this perfectly silent span of time, I remembered there was nothing like having loved ones around. It became clear to me the permanency of childhood impressions. So the story begins here, where everything was safe and familiar. And we thought then, that nothing could ever go wrong.

....

Grandma Arla and Grandpa Edwin fell ill a few weeks before the house was packed. While they were fighting to stay alive, they were also fighting with each other. Too stubborn and callous to let the other know, they never knew they were practically roommates admitted to the same hospital the same day, on the same floor.

Because of her stroke, Grandma never recognized Mom. Grandma would open and close her mouth in silence like a fish showing no emotion whatsoever. Grandpa never opened his eyes. Mom would travel from one room to the next, sit quietly with both of them and keep her mouth shut. She agreed that if either of them knew of each others' condition, it would only worsen the situation.

Only Damey, who was a year and a few seconds older than me, was allowed to view the lifeless bodies. Just wasn't fitting that a little lady like me see two sets of choppers floating around in a jar like a giganthopithecus ready to jump out and eat me during the bedside vigil.

Days later and only doors apart, Grandma and Grandpa both died. Surprised they'd be to find one another at the Pearly Gates as I'm quite sure Grandpa would never have made it there.

Grandpa was a mean old fart. His milky eyes, marinated in hops, kept his nose from sliding down onto his chin. I didn't know that the face he wore the few times he visited was his funny face or his real face and only Grandma and mom knew he wouldn't be staying for long. He smelled like a barrel of whiskey and had a day-old cigar dangling between his teeth that looked like rotten corn-on-the-cob. He steadied a knee for us to bounce, throw me over his shoulder like I was a lady's handbag, and balance me across his legs affording me ten pungent minutes, putting in his grandpa time before leaving to find his drink.

Grandpa didn't remember starving his own children when they were young, Mom, her sister Sally, and brothers Bobby and Eddy. My guess is that Grandpa didn't even remember having children at all. There was barely a smidgen for anyone to eat, unless the church folk managed to save them some on Sunday. Mom, Uncle Eddy, Aunt Sally and Uncle Bobby had bellies empty enough to touch their backbone. It was all too much for Grandma to bear. Grandpa had robbed them of food, money and dignity and disappeared for periods of time that tunneled into days and then weeks. Eventually he never came back at all. Until he remembered to die.

Grandma, on the other hand, never wanted to leave, didn't want to go and surely would've liked to kick grandpa's sorry ass if she could, had it not been for her babies. She was as lonely as a lily in a deserted pond. I remember her wearing the same grease-stained apron one day into the next after a double shift at the diner six days in a row. She had a sadness in her face, eyebrows fastened together in an enormously tight arch showing the aches and pains of her daily struggles.

Grandma's children became frail and weak over time, anemia had a way of brittling their bones and stealing their youthful spirit. With no other choice, Grandma had to put her four hungry mouths into an orphanage where she knew they would have a bed and a meal. They had already been left behind by Grandpa and found this to be no different. But it was their hunger that propelled them to go. All the colors of the rainbow couldn't replace the colorless months that lay ahead without a brother's familiar voice, the scent of a mother's presence or the feel of a sister's comforting hand during a rainstorm. They could now only glance at one another through a wired fence on all four corners of the compound. In their separateness, each child hunkered down with other lonely orphaned children their age, weeks stretching into months with no end in sight. Until two years later when Grandma earned enough money to bring her children home again.

....

After the funeral, Mom had little left of her roots in Parma and leaving her siblings behind, Dad decided to make our home many miles away from this place we had grown. We all climbed into the Mustang Convertible, Hutch, Damey, Schottzee the wiener dog and myself and headed for New York City.

Having bucket seats left a big lump in the middle of the backseat. Being the only girl between two slices of brother, one older, one younger, I was graciously awarded that position. God-forbid the dog got there first. Then I would have to share a huge lump with a long dog who had a tongue that looked exactly like a piece of thinly-sliced ham. I had bitten it once just to see if it was a piece of ham. It wasn't.

The windows in the Mustang were left open during the endless trek. The hills and treetops bobbed up and down hypnotizing us in moments of silence. To break the monotony, Damey managed to blow a few wind sonatas using the massive gap between the two front teeth that would no doubt, make a beaver jealous. He screeched winded breaths that sounded a bit like an old Broadway musical…changing the score to fit his lisping tongue and belching out words that had something to do with two gangs of hoodlums called the sharks and the jets.

"When you're a chet, you are always a chet, from your firth thigarette till your lath dying day." He had taken twelve jerk lessons, a dance of the sixties which enabled the upper torso to sway and snap back and forth as if possessed by the devil. He boasted of these theatrical abilities of which he had none. But we had learned long ago to shake our heads and ignore him.

Damey was good at instilling fear between Hutch and myself. He could purse and tighten his lips into one long hyphen, scrunch his eyes into a darting stare that sent daggers from within while mumbling the heart-pounding music from "The Man with the Wooden Leg," a story he had made up after breaking his leg in three places. He belted out a hair-raising "clump-ugh, clump-ugh," grab any part of Hutch, twist him into a contorted mess all the while "clump-ughing" himself into submission. And all he had to do to me was wriggle a Damey finger my way as if to tickle me unmercifully, setting me into a frenzy, without even a touch.

"I'm gonna get ya. I'm gonna tear you up with both a ma teeth. Then I's gonna spit you out like dog food... huummm." Then, like a ventriloquist barely moving his lips, grabbed my shoulders and wriggled his fingertips again. Wasn't particularly what I had in mind for twelve hours in the backseat of a Mustang Convertible with a lump and a dog with a meaty tongue.

I may have weathered the craggy claws, the poke, the prodding and the pestering screams. I could have lived through the jabs of crusty toes tickling my backbone. I could have done it all twice maybe, if it weren't for the pee jar. Dad wouldn't stop the car as long as there were empty pickle jars under the seat, and not even the Queen Mum herself could qualify a pit stop. Each time I had to hide behind a curtain of blankets, place myself on top of the opening with one hand, push the peering eyes away with the other, miss the hole completely and pee on Schottzee the wiener dog who tried to stick her curious long nose into my groin to see what the fuss was all about.

"Get that dog outta there." Swat! Mom, now annoyed at the urine circus in the back, missed Damey's knee knocking the dog down instead. So far, Schottzee enjoyed the trip even less than we did, poor girl. Damey folded his arms into a tight cross and took on a mouthy pout.

"Why can't you just pee in the jar like the rest of us?" he howled full of himself, as if he alone had masterminded the art of jar-pissing.

"Move over so your sister can take off those wet clothes," Mom demanded reaching behind from the front seat to pull them off. With the stench of urine and the humidity bowling us over, we hung the wet clothes between the roof and half-closed window for the passing wind to dry them. All I could think of was to crawl next to Hutch, still sculpted into a pretzel and hide while my underpants twisted in the wind for everyone to see and would surely recognize them as mine.

Hutch was less of an exhibitionist than Damey and had fooled our parents with his silent manipulation. He was fragile and skinny and occupied little space. His enormous ears flopped around like flags blowing in a slow wind. Had he been any lighter, he may have mysteriously floated out of Damey's window and been lifted up and away like a hovercraft. Damey of course, would have absolutely no knowledge of that whatsoever.

"Do your ears hang low, do they wobble to and fro? Can you tie them in a knot, can you tie them in a bow?" we'd sing. Hutch was not amused.

Time had a funny way of passing in the back with a lump and a long dog. Dad clutched the steering wheel looking straight ahead and talked to himself. He learned to shut us all out and entertain the crap out of himself. Never had I seen anyone arguing with themselves, then agreeing with himself all in the same breath. But there he was pondering his own question, rubbing his front tooth with his forefinger, nodding his head with pleasure then growling at himself when the first thought didn't agree with the second.

"I'll have Bud take on the Wendy's account...no, no, absolutely not...what am I thinking?" shaking his head with an incoherent "Yeah, that's what we'll try first," then concluding himself with a chuckle and grin that by now brought us over the border of Ohio into Pennsylvania. Dad was the only one I knew that could keep himself stimulated, occupied and thoroughly entertained with not a living soul around.

Nevertheless, I sat in the back, thanking the Almighty Lord, Jesus God, Himself, when the boys on each side of me fell asleep. I laid my head back against a pillow and watched the toiling landscapes whizzing by. The terrain became as flat as a dead man's EEG and left a deserted lifeline. The air conditioner flowed with a loud hum dampening our already dull mood. Occasionally a pickup truck tooled alongside us nodding in Mom's direction. Everyone looked at Mom.

Mom had the face of an Egyptian queen. Her eyes were dark and sullen and gave off the mystique of sexual allure. They were as syrupy as a Johnny Mathis Christmas song and could stare you down with loving praise, or malicious intent. Those were the eyes that tamed the intrigue in my Father's heart. (Years later, when gravity pulled on Mom's eye lids, she had cosmetic surgery to lift them back into place. She became ecstatic at conquering what might have been a debilitating facial blunder. Dad was smitten by her now as he was when seeing the youthful slip of the girl he had married years before. As for me, I thought she would never blink again.) Anyway, when the truckers weren't looking at my panties flapping for surrender, they were staring at Mom.

I watched the clouds darkening as the day dissipated. It seemed to cast a spell on us through the windows. I was drifting off as I waited for the evening sun to set. We drove on and I could see what the birds see, the great mountains against the clouds, perfectly cushioned above our heads. As the warm sunset slipped into night like a newborn slips into slumber, the skies danced an azure blue so like the color of my Father's eyes. The reflections off the small lakes we had been hugging caused a magenta to swirl and dance in the heavens as if the angels were melting candles onto their majestic palettes, smearing them like pastels. My heart couldn't help but dance with them in this visual "pas-de-deux." I didn't know if God's painting was conspiring to soften my mood or the winds over the lakes were to invent a canvas of hues unlike what our fingers could ever create. Either way, it kept me still from the moments of the day and quietly kissed us all goodnight. We linked our young heads together falling gently into each other's lap and sank into slumber for the remaining hours of the trip.

....

At o-dark hundred, just before sunrise, the Mustang convertible headed into the outer rim of Manhattan. We had officially made our entrance leaving behind Cleveland and the Terminal Tower, the only skyscraper we had ever known outside of the travel placards at the matinee. Hours behind us was the only city in the Great US of A, where the Cuyahoga River caught fire, where lake Erie was filled with dangerous toxins floating and where the Mayor's wife canceled dinner with the First Lady so not to miss her bowling night. There was left the roots and families who stayed familiar and close, never to escape reality. Buddha once said: "There is no tomorrow without today, no joy without suffering, no birth without pain." Apparently Buddha never lived in Cleveland.

Our new life had become a tiny spot on a crowded map with endless blocks of six lane streets and pedestrian cat walks. The Mustang cruised with caution as five sets of eyes, round as cantaloupes stared up at the high rises, all built within inches of each other, smothering any breeze in between.

Manhattan was a startling image of itself, art imitating life, birthing right before us. Broken remnants of buildings, windows with shards of glass littered the expressway, while the unforgiving stench of garbage filled our morning. Heat ghosted off the walls and stuck to the sidewalks making the air taste like lead. Sirens whistled constantly, barely leaving a moment to think. Trucks and cabs moved at high speeds slowing down just enough to knock into each other. Grand Central Station shuffled the same crowds to and from the trains like robots fully wound and tuned, bunching them together as they rotated around city blocks in and out of corporate structures, all in the hopes of hurrying through their day. Graffiti led the eye in and out of the back alleys, a flamboyant interlocking of self-expression. Every culture, every race, language and continent was there integrating itself in one way or another, and seemed to have followed our green Mustang from their piece of the globe to here, just to welcome us in.

We arrived at our destination, the Eden Apartments. This was Sol, the doorman's territory. Propped up on a three-legged bar stool at the entrance, Sol filled his days swiveling back and forth like he was balancing his entire torso on a pole stuck all the way up from his ass.

"Good Morning, pretty lady. May I assist you?" Sol opened the entrance door for Mom.

Sol took pride in his job. He was a big, burly man with a balding forehead brewing a faucet of sweat that shined through the heat. He had an unintentional three-day growth fertilizing his face and a scorpion tattoo on his left bicep which he kept hidden under his starched white shirt. When he flexed his muscle it was like it would jump out at you and latch itself onto your nose if you happened to poke your head in too close. Surprisingly, Sol had an endearing quality which captured not only Mom's heart, but the hearts and wallets of many lonely women. His dentures, as massive and gold as a fortress, gleamed a star quality smile that would make an accordion jealous.

Sol took an instant liking to Mom. Everyone took an instant liking to Mom. He never bothered with the rest of us to see if we needed any help. No, he didn't pull the red locks on my hair, or wiggle Hutch's ears or even acknowledge Dad, who unloaded the eleven bags of luggage all by himself. No, we were just about as exciting as freeze-dried water and Sol made sure we knew it.

Mom gave Sol a hard-on when gifting him with an ice cold beer every day at noon. Sol was born in the earthy Midwest himself and could relate to Mom's back home generosity. They quickly became friends by one o'clock and both were tipsy by three.

As for us kids, Sol wanted nothing more than to fill our young heads with his own concoction of mischief from the Bronx. What else were we to do in a neighborhood of cement, with people living so close together like grapes in a bunch.

"Tell ya's what kids. If ya's trow some water off ya's balcony up there, I jes bet ya's cool off dem young bucks down yonder walking by tinkin' dey is so impotent in dem linen suits and v-neck sweaters…faget about it…what idiot wears sweaters in da summer anyway." Sol mixed his Midwestern hoodlum with his Manhattan magic.

"Really Sol? We can dump water on them? I mean, won't we get in trouble?" I replied to the dare, wondering what else it is you do in a metropolis as this.

"Ya betcha there Hutch," forgetting about me.

"But first go get your mama to get me one of dem ice cold brews, now could ya, cowgirl?" Back to me.

"And get dat god-dang finger outta your nose before you poke your eye out, young fella," he snapped at Damey while swiping the sweat off his own brow with an Eden Apartment handkerchief.

Sol rolled up his sleeve to scare us with his scorpion for the fourteenth time since we moved in, only a day and a half ago just to hear us gasp.

Needless to say, we believed Sol. We believed everything Sol told us. Why wouldn't we? Anyone with a tattoo of a scorpion had to know something we didn't know. We were at the age between imbecile and idiot and everything sounded ripe and good for the picking to us. Simply put, Sol became the focus of our pathetically dull world in a city that never sleeps and truth be told, that was just fine with us.

Then there was Dad. Anything was possible with Dad. He's the guy by the way, that gave me those Bahamian blues, eyes clear enough to see ten feet within, You could probably see the wildlife in them if the pupil hadn't gotten in the way. And what with those tangled red circles hanging loosely off my head, I was just like Dad. My curiosity gyrated around inside my crimson head like a tilt-a-whirl too thanks to the Irish man with the red face.

"Who's gymnasium, Dad?" No answer. Dad would only gesture his impatience by rolling his eyes upwards planting them there for a second before bending his head into a sarcastic tilt waiting for me to answer my own question. "Who's that? What's this? Where ya going?"

"Couldn't she shut up for five minutes?" I'm sure he was thinking. I was a never-ending source of irritation to him. But to me, I could peer into his aquamarine irises and feel like a rushing tide in a tsunami of ambition. Dad was everything to me.

Dad acted as if every day was a new day, every day started on its own, everyday was Monday. He was a small town artist adapting to the hottest city of advertising in the world. He conjured up an atmosphere of sameness for us. Gone in the morning, home at night, jogging in and out as if to catch up to his own back end. We could only watch him in awe and hope he eventually noticed that we were still here.

"Men display their courage, while women practice patience." Dad referred to this often. I knew this to be true after hearing it so many times. Mom, Hutch, Damey, Schottzee the wiener dog and myself were the remaining souls on the vessel "Hopelessly Bored." Sol, still sporting a woody, kept an eye on Mom. His real one. Unfortunately for Sol he lost his left eye to a swift kick in the face in a bar room brawl. We had learned to focus on the good eye when it wasn't inconspicuously moving back and forth for the ladies passing by. But there we were, Damey growing upwards and swelling from the heat, Hutch wanted to burst from the invisible prison bars of the tiny city spaces and as for me, well it had taken me all summer to understand that I didn't understand any of it.

When summer finally melted away the home in Connecticut became available. For a second time in three months, we loaded up the green Mustang, crunched, nudged, bunched, kicked and screamed our way into the back seat, positioned ourselves for the post-war in the back seat and drove the hour to our new home.

....

Coming from the goiter capital of the world, Grayton, Connecticut was a culture shock. Progress, innovation, trend-setting, one would say, if looking for that sort of thing. It was the breeding grounds for the famous and hotbed for the sophisticated. The inhabitants were quite immune to the antiquated values we trolled in behind us from the Midwest.

The small town was camouflaged within her trees. The colors of the leaves as autumn rolled in created rich golds and bronze blanched by heat blending together as if Monet had painted the entire landscape just for our amusement. It was dressed in colonial charm, pine, evergreens and distant hills surrounding privately-owned lakes. It had fireplaces and ski slopes and windy two-lane roads hidden beneath the tapestries of greens, reds, bronze and golds as far north as the eye could stretch.

The beaches bordered the Long Island sound. The surf invented her own mood while a subdued low tide was set in for the seagulls to shoot down like kamikaze bombers to the open prey on the jetties peeking out from the waves. There were remnants of the Revolutionary War along the shoreline. An iron-cast colonist with his three-cornered hat and musket at arm's length stood next to the cannons guarding the beaches. The inscription beneath the canon's barrel was clear. "Here We Guard Our Beaches." I'm sure some smart ass etched that on there since the original etching was worn from the weather. Regardless, we were content to know those iron guys and massive cannons kept our beaches safe.

Down the road was our new home. Terrace Lane was framed with pine trees and wound about concealing itself in the brush. The house was perched on a lot overlooking what we thought to be a forest coming from a street with only one tree, three acres of dense pines and swampy ponds, alluding to a portrait of quiet magnetism. This is where we called home.

The house was cozy and warm. Embers simmered in the fireplaces from late autumn to early spring. Even now I can smell the scent of the logs cindering that first autumn and see the wind funneling the leaves up in a spherical shape like those drawn in an animated cartoon. I can smell the cider and the apples plucked from their harvest outside our door and still savor the tart of its first bite. All the colors of New England return to me in these moments. Stretching this moment even further, I have the blanketed feeling that nothing could interrupt its beauty.

We arrived ahead of the moving truck. The foliage rustled their welcoming arms all around us. We immediately explored the new environment. The house was a distance from the main road up the hill and so we all, Damey, Hutch, Schottzee and myself scattered into different directions.

"A guy could get lost in these woods," Damey announced his plans as he dashed out of the back seat. Damey just couldn't sit still even if a gun barrel was pointed at his head, so he was the first to dart into the backyard like a bullet.

"Get lost then. For good. And don't come back," Hutch muttered under his breath. Hutch was more inclined to take cover behind Mom before Damey could squeeze his elephant ears with the bony nodules he called fingers. Hutch would have done anything to trade him in for an improved version of big brother instead of the one he wanted to feed to the lions just for sport. Instead he prided himself on nasty comments, although barely audible, hoping Damey had heard him wrong before disappearing again.

Obviously, this was a happy time. Just ask Schottzee the wiener dog. If she could show her bliss, she would have giggled a lot. The smile drawn below her wiener dog nose was always turned up as if she were laughing right along with us. She wagged her tail furiously and peed.

"Schottzee made a river," Grandma May would announce nonchalantly thinking it quite natural to laugh and pee at the same time. May was a lot like Schottzee the wiener dog, giggling and peeing. May was her name and what everyone called her. Never Grandma, never Mom, auntie or Mrs. Somebody. Only May.

Grandma May visited us three times a year from Ohio. Here she joined us for the first time as we moved into the new house. She was the only souvenir from home and although she took on the role of the inspector general most times, she became a pleasant addition in our new life. She had already raised her two sons, Dad and Uncle Riso after Grandpa's heart imploded, well before Dad was barely thirteen and was here now to look after us.

May blanketed us with stories of her life growing up holding us close to her large bosom. Over the years her boobs sagged so much landing just above her belly button, taking on the appearance of socks with quarters in them. Having lost their flare and purpose, she no longer cared to hide them as much and we found them to be a great source of comfort when huddling around her for a "May tale," or in other words, a fabricated version of anything that popped into her sparkling bluish-white little Irish head.

May had reveled in the freedom of her youth, living independently well into her thirties. Up until World War II, unmarried women were objects of pity. On the contrary for May, who gloated on the wild wolf living inside her she felt as if she were singing and dancing with the rhythm of the wind, running congruent with the tides, lighting the fires that sizzled in the hearts of the brave men overseas.

Only after the men went to fight for their country, and the women began to run the household and raise the children alone, and only when mothers drilled the screws into tanks and soldered wings onto aircraft and bombers and munitions, utilizing their slender fingers to shape and mold the tools of war, did the boundaries for unmarried women expand. There was no longer the stigma of the poor unlucky lady who never was taken, never wed and would never have children. Only the satisfaction of female presence and strength, of unity and power to carry on alone. Men would later appreciate this so suffice it to say, May was well ahead of her time.

I had come to respect May not for her gender, but her strengths and talents. May was straight-forward and curt and yet could never stay mad. She absorbed the joys and pains of others as if they had were pathways into her own journey. She would pucker up an angry yelp, all the while her diamond-shaped, aqua blue eyes, the watery kind you can see right through, twinkled like limericks in a poem. Her anger turned into a chuckle one chuckles when laughing at themselves. So it was no surprise that everyone wanted to be around her.

Even Schottzee stood at May's feet looking up at her in an adoring sort of way. Every now and again, they would glance at each other, Schottzee and May, grandma and dog, checking out their karmic connection.

May had other talents, too. She could laugh and fart at the same time. They just slipped out loud enough to make one jump defying all fart logic. She called them "toots" but we never heard a French horn do that before. May was literally a walking body of gaseous air, had little bladder control, a wealth of humor and a psychic connection to a dog. I adored her.

....

Most of our time outside of school was spent at Alex's house. Alex's family had moved from another midwestern town to Grayton only two months before we arrived. Both of our families were overwhelmed by Grayton's rather unusual social design.

Turney Road encircled itself like a runaway shoe lace. Its winding curves had horse ranches and dairy farms leading smack into Alex's dead end drive.

Alex's house stood for nearly a century, worn and torn from the transient drug addicts who tried their hand at drug rehabilitation years before the family moved in. It was a rotoundly massive piece of architecture with side columns reaching upwards as if to grab onto God's tethering line. The iron gate at the bottom of the drive bordered the entrance that lead to this ominous structure. Sometimes at dusk, when the lemon colored sun was hiding behind the trees and a vacant cloud, and a mist was borrowed from the afternoon rain, you could almost feel as if you were a guest to a ghostly mansion finding every step you take to be a cautious one. It became a playground and intrigued us to no end.

The "big house" was what everyone called it. When someone was lost they were either in the big house, or holding on to dear life in the pool in the back yard. There was always someone running in and out of the kitchen, that in itself occupied the entire rear of the house. Or they sought anonymity in the attic to spin around on the antique barber shop chairs from the junkies stay at rehabilitation.

Many stormy afternoons were spent up there watching the trees outside the wired windows throwing tantrums to the nasty winds. This was sometimes more menacing than the creepy child ghosts with jet black hair creeping up the stairs to the blackness like bugs fusing into the night, and slip around the corner to spy on whoever was hiding there first. The light illuminated their faces while their high-pitched shrills screamed out...."AHHHAAA," as if they had caught us snorting a gun barrel of cocaine rather than puffing on the snubbed-out stale cigarette butt we had found the week before.

Sometimes we would all be hiding up in the attic at the same time, which turned out to be hiding from no one at all. What with thirty pounds of crimson locks and forty pounds of imagination, it was all I could do to keep from thinking I had gone through a portal into a mystical land of surprises in this magnificent broken down palace. But over time, no one knew who was missing on any particular day and eventually found no purpose in their escapade. They simply returned to the thunderous crowds downstairs in the "big house" and life went about as usual.

....

One day, a man, a very unusual man, a man with no children, no family, no connection whatsoever to a lifeline to the living, moved in. He rented out the garage turned cottage and he became the first tenant in hopes of relieving the financial burdens of a large family in a large home housing two adults, twelve children and all of their closest friends, which by now, nobody bothered to count anymore.

His name was Haddi Grimace. Haddi brought with him his own concoction of mischief, ironically kin to our boredom and we all tagged along together. Our listlessness finally had a name.

No one really liked Haddi Grimace. No one really disliked him either. Actually, no one could figure him out. He dwelled within the boundaries of his own mind. He had no logic as to which direction he was headed although he always ended up somewhere. His real identity mystified even himself. Haddi was an array of genius and slug, fact and fantasy. He painted portraits of nudes and backdrop scenery for the local playhouse. Haddi thought fornication had something to do with bran cereal and long walks in the park, therapy and recovery. So it was no surprise Haddi had only one friend.

"Twinkie was her name, and don't you forget it!" Haddi would chuckle as if he was having an orgasm just thinking about her. "Twinkie will always be next to my heart," he muttered as he pretended to pat her love letter into his chest, although his heart must have been in his ass because the letter that was supposed to be in his shirt pocket was forever peeking out of his back pocket instead. Here's what it said....

"Sup, Yo, Yo, Haddi. My name is Twinkie and I am happier than a pig-in-shit to be released in two weeks from the Northwest Women's Correctional Institute and now looking for love. I would've stayed married to Bubba but being that he is now locked up for trying to off the President, he's been having a real hard time getting that 48 hour pass for good behavior. So at this point Haddi, I am hornier then a six-toed cat.

Truth be told Haddi, I kinda needed the break so those gray walls came in handy. See in some prisons for us gals, we get to keep our babies for up to a year if they are born inside these prison bars. Lucky for me, I had all 13 of my brats before I got there. I'll be damned if I was gonna miss American Idol on account of a crying kid.

Got some help there too what with my wooden leg and all. Yep, free medical.....well, sorta free, if ya know what I mean, wink, wink. Banged my leg up big time when I crashed a motorcycle I stole when I was ten and ran it into a brick wall. But hey Haddi, I was young and stupid and what, at ten years old, didn't know which pedal was the brake or which brake was the pedal, oh you know what I mean. Okay, stupid I know. Better yet I am still able to use the metal plate in my head from that very same crash and lucky for me and all my new friends here in the tank, I can get HBO through my eyeballs.

And besides, Haddi, where else could I have gotten corn beef hash and a hard block of jello with one cherry in it at every meal? Who makes those blocks of jello anyway? And how in the heck do you get that cherry right smack in the middle of that thing? I want that job. Anyway, If you ask me it is more like a five-star hotel, ya know like the one on forty-fourth street, where the drunk guy behind the counter only falls off his stool after you pay the twelve bucks. Geez Haddi, life is good.

Anyway Haddi, sorry I don't have a picture yet but I am still waiting for the eczema to clear up on my scalp so my hair can grow back. So I hope to hear from ya soon lover boy, cause I know there is someone for everyone. Or at least here in the pokey, there is everyone for someone. Love, Twinkie."

Haddi considered Twinkie to be his only family, his only friend, his soul mate, his rose in a bed of weeds and he would read the letter over and over again rubbing his bony fingers over it like it was freshly spun silk, then sniffed the words as if they were as pungent as the dogwoods in spring. We learned later that Haddi and

Twinkie had never really met but he considered her his rare find and clung to the thought of someday banging the crap out of her.

Each morning before breakfast, Haddi did a hundred sit-ups. Never missed a day. He set the table at nine in the morning for the evening's meal in the cottage and wore his old ripped up bathrobe where his pajama pockets housed his portable phone in case anyone called him for a job.

"I can only work from twelve to one o'clock, with an hour off for lunch," he joked to us when we asked him who in fact would call? He bragged to everyone how busy he was but spent most of his time wandering the grounds wondering what it was he would do next.

"I have something more powerful than most men," Haddi delighted in his meaningless chatter. "It is large and flexible, could be swift or stiff. It can periodically explode but is always kept hidden away." Some thought it to be his penis, but by now, we knew it to be his imagination.

It was this imagination that pressed upon my memory of him. Always a scheme to brew or philosophy to draw from. He used fake accents when conferring on particularly absurd topics and went onto other stories using other fake accents.

"We were eighteen years old, Richard and I." Haddi began his life story one afternoon yelling at us from his window in the cottage above the pool. Haddi had just set the table for the next morning's meal, checked his phone and no one had called him, read Twinkies letter a dozen times, then ran out of things to do. He decided to roam to the "big house" for something to do. We all waited for him to jump into the pool with us for a good laugh but instead he decided to plant himself on the grass and stay dry. One by one, we got out of the pool and with a beach towel and sniffles we circled Haddi to hear one of his imaginary tales.

"Dick was 100% bon-a-fide trouble. He managed to talk me into hopping aboard the Queen Mary one morning, just before the old gal left San Francisco. He was good at jumping on and off the ladies," chuckle. Haddi kept our attention then began sizzling himself into a German dialect.

"Who's Dick?" I ask as I'm shivering from the cold and rubbing my ear full of water but knowing full well that when Haddi talks, everybody listens.

"Ve veer headed vor London, Vichard Krrranium and I." Haddi shook his head as if to unscramble the memories. He blinked his eyes twice and looked up as if to check inside his own forehead for the next sentence. We weren't quite sure if he was inventing the story as he spoke but let him go on anyway.

"Richard," he repeated this time in a British drawl. "We climbed aboard and cruised the upper decks just as it was leaving port." Haddi began chuckling himself into a full blown chortle as he began recapturing the day.

"Yeah, old Deeks-san-me," now adding a French twist.

"Who's 'deek-san-me?" Alex mimicked. Haddi shot a raised eyebrow and a dirty look at us.

"You neva inturrrrupt Haddi's kkrreative flaws."

"Flows, Haddi. Don't you mean creative flows?"

"Zat's vat I sad, flaws," back to German, this time gestapo-like.

Although it became clear that Haddi was in and out of his own delusions, we pressed harder and harder for him to go on.

"What, was the ship as big as a city like they say?" Alex's curiosity set in.

"Where did ya plan on sleeping?" I chimed in, wondering where it was all going.

"Well, we weren't planning on anything yet." Back to English where he didn't have to think so hard. "Unless of course, something presented itself to us. End it alvays doz in Haddi vorld," on to more German and annoying us to death. "First, we had to see what Queenie offered." Haddi acted as if the whole trans-Atlantic vessel was sailing the open waters just for this adventure.

"We couldn't get through the crowds at first, but when we slipped through the confusion and fumbled our way past the guy checking the manifest, we decided we had to eat something in case we were caught. We first found the galleys below deck, and Dick, that dick, ha, grabbed a chef's jacket on a hook near some boxes...tons of boxes, fish and fruits out the wazoo. I guess we could have just grabbed something right there but why do that when we could feast like everyone else? Wink. Hey, we got this far, didn't we?" He shot a full-fledged grin at us widening his eyes like he was opening the treasure chest to his mind.

"I followed Dick to the dining rooms. Aaaah, the crystal chandeliers, and the zzzrimp, zimp, imp, imp," almost a possessed stutter like his tongue fattened itself out for the next sentence.

"Shrimp, Haddi, shrimp. Knock it off." Haddi focused and tried again.

"Oh, the women, rich with desire for me and Dick, two Greek gods I must add." Another chuckle.

"We sauntered like two leopards in heat, greeting the guests, nodding and complementing our work." Another chuckle.

"What work, Haddi?" Alex hadn't recalled a job he had, or any work he had done for that matter.

"The food, work....we were the chef's, remember?"

"They didn't fall for it, did they?" I had to ask myself as I wondered how many imposters I might have come upon without knowing it.

"Wouldn't believe what rich people fall for." Haddi shook his head almost envious of what money can buy, fame, fine dining, young horny studs from Cleveland hopping aboard a ship.

"Would you like a crème Brulee' for dessert, Madame?" French, again. "And don't you look like a pearl tonight?" The women were astounded by our good looks, okay, fine, great looks, and obvious culinary skills. With an inviting wink, we removed their half-emptied plates from the table, walked with the finesse of a swan back to the galley, found a closet nearby and ate the leftovers."

"Eeeks." Our young minds were unable to grasp it all and we shivered at the thought of eating scraps like a dog.

"Oh no, these weren't just your ordinary scraps. These were the highest quality, Grade A, top of the line scraps."

"How was it no one saw you?" Alex and I crinkled our brows in suspense unsure as to whether to believe him or not.

"No one really noticed. All they noticed was the curve of our fine, and I mean FINE sculpted ass, not an ounce of grisle, mind you. You don't think I look Greek now do you?" Haddi posed turning his head to the side puffing up his chest and sucked in his cheeks and stuck out his tongue.

"No, Haddi....you look like a zipper. But do go on."

Even as young girls, growing into our sexual primes, we hadn't noticed Haddi to be any too handsome at all, and certainly no Greek God, or barely human for that matter. He was more like a character that jumped out of a fairy tale we had yet to read.

We had, however, noticed his eyes could speak a tale of adventure furiously blinking at times and it were those eyes that kept us spellbound as he continued on.

"There were so many people milling about the ship waiting on the on the fat, jeweled bastards. But as far as we were concerned, it was some of the best damn grub we ever ate."

Haddi took a seat on the grass and crossed his legs into a lotus position. He lifted his bottom up with his knuckles dug into the grass and farted. We had never seen that done before. The little ones who had gathered for the remainder of his stories ran away, having had enough of Haddi and his ocean voyage and ridiculous accents. The sun was retreating behind a rain cloud and gave us a shiver. It started to drizzle.

"Where' did ya sleep?" By now we had the attention of a goat, ready to chomp on anything.

"Depended."

"On what?" Our curiosities were saturated by now and we were about to believe anything he told us.

"On who was looking. We snuck a stogie from the smoking room that first night. Tasted like a meadow muffin but toked on it anyway."

"What's a meadow muffin?" I asked.

"It's a muffin in the meadow, smart one. Ya know, cow shit."

"Then Dick, I mean Deeeek," he added for effect, "crawled down behind the movie screen at the theater. Was getting dark and figured we needed to sleep off dinner and hideout the rest of the night. The kids watching the movie on the other side of the screen saw shadows as we spread out some blankets we found, wormy old things, got spooked and ran to find someone, little shits, and before Richard could 'blah-blah-blah' his way through who gets the woven American flag spread, there were security guys dressed like keystone cops come running around back to chase us down."

"Did you get away? Where did ya go?"

"Well I got away. It was kinda like a slapstick movie, guys running in from every corner, tripping over ropes and boxes until two guys grabbed Richard by the hair and almost pulled him right in half. Almost broke his fool neck, too, that dick head."

"Well, I would've gotten away," I said.

"Me too." Both Alex and I found ourselves in the story with him. We shivered at the excitement of it all.

"What did he do?"

Haddi shook his head back and forth, didn't stop, didn't say a word. Just shook and shook as if his cranial battery began dying out.

"What? So what, WHAT HAPPENED?, Haddi?"

"Richard charmed his way right out of their grip and into the ladies lounge. Told them he was the activities director or some hog wash tale like that. I found him later and he had two old farts waiting to bed us down. Now that's living ain't it?"

"Man-o-Man, Haddi, you could charm the skin off a rattlesnake, couldn't ya? Did you ever make it to London? Oh, I'm sorry, I mean Vondon." I was hooked into the accents while I giggled.

"Just before sunrise on the morning before we arrived into the London docks, a bulletin circulated about two stowaways on board the ship. WANTED: TWO AMERICAN STUDS....LADIES, KEEP YOUR POCKET-BOOKS CLOSE AND YOUR PANTS ON." Haddi chuckled himself silly with this until Alex broke his spell.

"Anyone you knew? Ha ha."

"That would be me, Professor. Like an idiot, Dick got real scared when they found out about us and jumped into the Atlantic, freaking-freezing ocean quarter mile offshore and swam right into the arms of the law. They were waiting right there for him. I wasn't so stupid."

At this point, Haddi stretched out and lay on the lawn which by now was dampened from the drizzling rain. The air tasted salty and the branches moved about as if applauding his wild adventure. Haddi lay full out, full of himself and the ease in which he had crossed the ocean, as he says, "at no cost, not even a coupon."

"I stayed aboard where it was warm and waited for the ole boys to cuff me as I walked off the ship with the other dastardly fools."

"Were you arrested?"

"Does a bear have boobs?, oh never mind. Yeah, we got arrested. Spent a night in the hole, too. Food ain't so good there. We did get a free ticket home though, compliments of the great United States of America. It was all over the newspapers here in the states. Didn't you read about it?" Haddi boasted this fact knowing full well this well before our time.

Anyway, Haddi thought surely we would think he was highly cultured. We thought him to be many people, and none of those people living inside his head were the least bit sane. But Haddi had us perplexed nonetheless. He, thus far, was the most amusing story in the small town of Grayton.

....

Haddi eventually earned the respect of the parents in the "big house." Everyone was welcome, as far as they were concerned. Haddi made them laugh so much sharing his adventures and his quirky philosophies at dinner that he could make up at a moment's notice.

"If you must, you must...If you will you will...the crow will come calling tomorrow. Or was that a turkey?" he would mutter to himself.

By now we didn't much care what he was saying only laughed at what he thought he might be saying even though it meant nothing to us at all. His colorful words that darted in and out of his reality became the bait when his eyes lit on fire as he spoke, arms flailing about in such an animated way pulling us closer into his hypnotic state. He was good. Very, very good.

"I have been called to prayer in the mosques," then speaking in tongue mimicking the Arabs while splitting a piece of rye bread in half. "Oh, and pass the pickles. P-I-C-K-L-E-S." He then smirked.

"I have dined with the kings of Egypt. I have kayaked in the fjords of the Netherlands," raising his eyebrows "with one arm behind my back. Good way to fall out...ha, even rode the ferris wheel at the Mall-of-America, woo-woo-mountain dew," he added to mock the Midwestern twang. Haddi couldn't contain himself and cupped his hands over his face, shoulders shaking in hysteria, until he drew a long breath before silencing himself.

Funny thing about Haddi. He thought he was the most hilarious person he had ever known. And that could very well be true being that he didn't know anybody, except Twinkie. We watched his animated ways unfolding right there before our eyes, dinner and a show, Haddi in the starring role. Nothing delighted us more than being around Haddi. His mind was a tilt-a-whirl of ideas. We thought him harmless and allowed him to run free inside the big house, helping himself to the channel changer and the chocolate coated Pop Tarts. Just another fixture along with all the ten children and their favorite friends, who by the way, like Haddi, never left for long.

Haddi did decide to leave one day and didn't return for quite a long time. For Haddi to venture out from the comforts of his curious audience was unusual, but at first no one noticed. We kept hiding in the attic or falling into the pool or spread ourselves around the grounds like commandos stalking the cottage until his return.

Three weeks passed before Haddi came back. He appeared in the kitchen one day as if no time had passed at all. He was unshaven and waif, his face taking on the color of oatmeal. The long bluish hair that circulated his empty scalp like a lasso was now hanging down on one side. The headband that kept the hair in place was now missing. It scared us at first, and we weren't sure if this was one of his characters emerging for the next show. But it certainly didn't bother him any, or maybe it would have if he was aware of it. Nevertheless, his appearance seemed of no consequence while he opened and closed the refrigerator door.

"I am trying to catch the light off," Haddi gestured us over to him to show us. The glowing expressions in Haddi's eyes when he spoke before he left was now gone. Perhaps he wasn't sleeping well.

"Yeah, he's back," Alex shrugged as we watched him caress the refrigerator door. "Something's up though, ya know what I mean? The old guy just ain't clicking these days."

I hadn't really said it but Alex and I both knew that something wasn't quite right. Haddi didn't have the insatiable energy he used to have. Even his piercing blue eyes were swelling out like pin cushions. Haddi left the kitchen and paced about the yard in a meditative state, back and forth, back and forth like a Tibetan monk in prayer. We were becoming increasingly aware of his mood swings. His bloodshot eyes glassed over when we got close enough to see into them. Haddi would stop in mid-sentence as if he never meant to speak at all, leaving his mouth at half-mast.

Alex and I watched him from the porch swing while he paced from one side of the pool to the next, raising his arms towards the sky and craning his neck forward and back responding to something that only he could hear. Alex and I watched dumbfounded.

"Can you hear that? What, the..." Alex asked.

"Yeah, I hear my heart pounding is what I hear. He's gotten weird. I mean worse weird. Do you think he has voices in his head?" I had always wondered what was actually living in his head with him but now it was becoming apparent that I wasn't too far off in my suspicions.

Alex and I never stopped looking at him and were a bit nervous as to whether we should strike up a conversation. We were not used to Haddi's silence and quite honestly had missed his blubbering himself silly about one thing after another. We had come to expect odd moments in the presence of Haddi, but nothing quite this strange.

Alex's mom, having birthed ten children, being a devout Christian and sharing her kindness with other strange people in her lifetime, found nothing out of the ordinary at first. She was used to odd. Who wouldn't be with so many people mingling around the house all day long. So she kept right on singing her hymns of praise to the Lord.

"I thank thee Lord for my daily bread.
I thank thee Lord for a warm, soft bed.
I thank thee Lord for these songs in my head.
Oh my Lord, I thank you."

On and on she'd praise, as if the day would never end. God was always on her tongue and on her mind. Mama, as everyone called her, was probably the happiest person on God's green earth. There was nothing that was ever said or done to her or her family, that wasn't the Lord's wishes and a guaranteed pathway to Heaven. The good Christian that she was, brought her closer to the right arm of God and in knowing this every day, she knew she was just another step closer to paradise. Her songs of joy and happiness spread like cool whip throughout the household and it came as no surprise that everyone felt safe when she was around.

Mama wished to fill our young lives with God's words and danced her way through the house that day, like every other day, in pure admiration for her Lord and life itself. But today would prove to be different.

Time went on and Haddi began to speak again, or growl one might say.

"I have found myself." Haddi yelled this from across the lawn. "I have FOUND MYSELF, my true inner being," exaggerating the words to make the meaning more clear.

"Were you lost?" I yelled back with a giggle as if to coerce him into saying more.

"I have reached nirvana..N-I-R-V-A-N-A. My mind is a cavern of love, a well filled with the deepest of understanding, life's mysteries, if you will....retoric, retoric, r-e-t-o-r-i-c."

"Retor-what? You twisted ball of freak," I mouthed the words so he couldn't hear me.

"My words come from him." Haddi bellowed this out as if we knew who him was and what it all meant.

Back and forth again he strolled head bowed, arms connected behind his back.

"Who's him?" I asked Alex completely out of breath.

"One of his imaginary friends, I guess." Alex and I looked at each other in utter amazement.

"I thought we were his only friends?" I asked.

"It doesn't count when you make 'em up."

We had been winded from scrambling from the porch swing to slither down a stone wall to spy on Haddi. We were now beginning to think this was just another one of his personalities and soon we would be sitting by the pool listening to another story.

Haddi became more peculiar as the days passed, placing himself somewhere else on the grounds, squatting behind trees or spread eagle on the stone wall. He would meditate for hours then suddenly wake and chuckle out loud. His mouth stuck wide open when he roared with laughter and then was silenced between gurgles as if he had to remember what was so funny in the first place.

Days went on and there was more chatter and meditation. Then Haddi began to move about pacing the lawn and decided one afternoon to follow Alex and I upstairs to her bedroom. We scrambled through the door and locked it behind us when he reached the last flight of steps. Haddi stopped just short of it before bumping into the door jam and began chanting his words of heresy.

"My love for you goes through doors. My love for you goes through walls. My love for you will never stop," and caressed the door with both arms from the opposite side.

"Love who?" We both said in unison. We didn't even know he loved us at all.

"You cannot escape me for I am everywhere. There are none so blind, as those that do not see." He was relentless.

We climbed onto the top of a chair and tried to spit on his head through a small window above the door, a half-hearted attempt to put out his psychic fires. Alex tipped the chair and we both fell with a crash onto the bed. Haddi pounded louder on the door and we could do nothing but run, this time to a bathroom that led out a different door. Nobody was laughing anymore.

"Leave us alone, you sadistical shit," Alex screamed half-giggling, half scared out of her wits.

"You cannot hide from me. You cannot hide from my master. My master is one. We will find you wherever you go." He continued to yell this repeatedly, frothing at the mouth. He held his arms straight up into the air and swung them back and forth like a buoy in a storm.

Mama was becoming disturbed and confused thinking that perhaps Haddi was only testing her Christian faith. She grew unsure of his intentions and soon began to realize, after his relentless pursuit of mockery, that he was not here to tease them but to overcome the household with his demonic delusions.

Haddi was traipsing deeper into a psychotic episode. His irrational mind began tangling in its own debris. He hummed a mantra from soft to loud. A hungry panther was growing inside of him. The daggers in his eyes felt as if he would cut us from our skins. He disguised his words as love and his blank expression made us feel as if something more diabolical than I had imagined was swimming around inside of his head.

The depth of his madness was becoming too real. Haddi was intent on dancing with the devil and saw it fit that we join him.

The kitchen was one floor below the bedroom and yet Mama still heard the banging. She began to pray, sing, yell at the Lord as she jogged towards the staircase to check the commotion upstairs.

"Lord, God, please remove this man, this Satan from my home," she yelled out as Alex and I ran by.

"Jehovah, save these children," begging to Him by now, anything she could do to get His attention. She had never found God to be a negligent God only an absent one by now. It would take days for God to hear her prayers and have Haddi removed from the home. But not before he had his way with the devil he referred to as "Master."

Haddi left the second floor and returned to the kitchen where everyone began to gather. His eyes glazed over as he darted past the doorway to the living room. He searched each corner, from left to front then left again. He began stampeding back and forth grabbing anything of value off the fireplace mantle and out of the closets nodding his head in approval of his finds. He gathered the oil paintings off the walls and while balancing them under one arm, ran back to the kitchen.

"I will sacrifice for my Master. I will give him what is his." Haddi bolted out his plan. "I sail on the forbidden seas. There is no point in having no point at all." Haddi stammered not knowing everyone was standing in stone cold fright wondering what the heck he was talking about.

"There is no pain for those who do not feel." His arms began to waver as he sputtered out garbled quotes. I listened to him hoping this was something my imagination was exaggerating and waited for the fires to dim.

He walked back to the foyer, then the dining room again, searching, a crazy man on a mission. He took the candlesticks off the table and saw himself in the reflection. Before he caught himself from the lull of the moment, he ran back, threw the candlesticks to the side and shoved the paintings on top of the stove and lit the burners.

Haddi, slowing down almost osmotizing into another personality, then sauntered into the library. His eyes glazed over like donut holes and again he looked upwards as if his evil spirit had hooked him into hypnosis and guided his way.

Mama by now gathered the children and placed them outside of the house while screaming over the telephone for help. Alex and I stood as human shields in front of the little ones as we pushed them out the door, our mouths agape at the madness we were witnessing.

Haddi then returned to the kitchen with the tapestries, heirlooms from Mama's Grecian ancestors and placed them on top of the burning fire. He revealed his instructions that were rolling around inside his head, an indistinguishable chatter upon his quivering lips.

"I give these things to you my Master, with fire to burn, burn, burn."

Within seconds, the flames declared a question mark that swirled from the kitchen to the dining room. A fiery waltz, a smothering baroque of black smoke spread to the ceiling and encased the spiraling stairs. Haddi chanted deliriously, satanic rubies rolling off his tongue as a symphony of flames danced from wall to wall like a scaly dragon breathing zigzags of fire. White ribbons of smoke poked through the roof and laced the sky.

Haddi became paralyzed. He stood in the midst of the heat and stared at the flames as they careened around him. He sang the song again, he had heard over and over on the radio.

"FIRE, I BID YOU TO BURN," and then mimicked a drum roll with his tongue.

"I will seek you and find you and give to you, my, master." He clenched his teeth and growled and salivated like a rabid dog. Haddi had not felt the need to save himself and continued making furious love with his words while singing his songs.

Mama ran to the back of the house for air choking and screaming at the same time.

"GET OUT OF MY HOUSE, YOU MONSTER...DAMN YOU TO HELL!" She was never one to raise her voice unless clambering out a song of worship and now clear as the northern ice, whipped Haddi with a rope and cursed at high volume, with the devil himself.

We all ran up the hill with her. It was all we could do to unfurl our brow at the work of a psychopath and come to grips that none of us had been consumed yet by the smoke. We watched as the house became Haddi's sacrificial torch, fulfilling his ego to no end as we waited for help to arrive.

Haddi, the most amusing character in Grayton, the man we had grown to admire, the man who had filled us with tales of the world, an enigma in his own right, was taken away in a straight-jacket that day. God had finally arrived.

The house simmered for three days. The furniture, the statuettes, the Persian rugs gave way to soot and a charring skeletal frame. Our fantasies and lore, our dancing and laughter died with the house and our ashes sealed our youthful bliss. What was previously unnamed was now spoken for, in his words, his touch, his actions.

That was the end of our life in Grayton. Two weeks later on moving day, Damey, Hutch, Mom, Dad and myself climbed into the same green Mustang convertible that brought us here years before. Leaving the wealth and charm of Grayton, the ocean and the toxicity of a privileged life and headed back to the manicured tree lawns and chrome balls.

Alex stood standing like a statue in freeze-tag when we drove up the long driveway to the "big house" to say goodbye. She watched us as I hugged the little ones and cried, then boarded the car with our waves of farewell.

The older brothers and sisters, my childhood mates stood behind her, like a set of stairs, one behind the other, legs in a triangular fashion with hands behind their back amidst a background of soot.

I had spent almost every day there for what seemed a lifetime at this house and to part with it now had never crossed my mind a month before. I watched the family I had grown up with, had spent all my joy and secrets with and was thinking this moment was quite possibly the saddest moment of my young life.

It surpassed the death of my gaseous grandmother, May, who had died of a heart attack six months before and right up there with the wrench of a wounded heart when Schottzee the wiener dog was found drowned.

Six months before, Schottzee had slipped into a neighbor's pool that had been covered with vinyl for the winter. It had collected weeks of rain and melted snow and she had fallen into it, exhausting herself literally to death in trying to climb back out. How ironic it was that May had passed on from a heart attack at the same time Schottzee fell into the pool. And now the house that built my youth and memories was gone.

I had earned my place in the front seat of the Mustang. Mom forfeited her position next to Dad and climbed into the back because of my reluctance to leave. But mostly it was so I could stretch my fingertips to Alex's after quietly waving goodbye. Alongside the car we touched tip to tip as she followed us down until every inch of the driveway was behind us. No one wanted to see my sobbing or recognize my broken heart. The front seat gave me the power to look only ahead not to the side or back. As we drove down the long winding driveway, everyone fell silent.

And there we were heading back home to Ohio, where everyone stayed together through eternity, where life was safe, warm and familiar. But especially, where nothing could ever go wrong.

In Irish Hopes

The television was continually on and kept everyone from talking to one another, should they unexpectedly have something so say. The white carpet lay under the piano and the overstuffed couch. There lay Mom asleep, television so low that only her breathing stirred the vacancies around her.

I noticed that Mom wept more and spoke less, sinking into a blackness every evening right about the time we all arrived home from high school. Frozen dinners were pulled from the freezer as if she had thought about doing that all day. She tried to shake herself awake. I asked her how her day had been and only a blank stare followed as if I had said nothing at all.

Mom had grown thin and frail, her face taking on the color of cornmeal. Those Egyptian eyes that illuminated and drew men from afar in happier days were now drawn and weak, the graceful twinkle gone.

Mom would stare at me as only a mother could penetrate a child's eyes only to tune me out and focus on my brow. In her silence I had hoped she would pave a passageway for me to enter deep inside her mind. Her jawbone, once defined in artistic splendor, drooped now showing only sadness. I had not seen this look since grandma & grandpa died years ago. I wanted to know where she was at in that very moment. But I never did.

Mom began drinking herself into oblivion. She needed a campfire to get her through her lonely nights and found it in cheap liquor and a shallow glass. She seemed to be chasing after shadows but could never find the sun. She was a single blade in a meadow of seed. She spent the next eight years wading down a stream, sinking and floundering like a trout trying to find its way downstream, she was between the two doors of depression and despair. Like a father who chose to drink himself to death and a mother too poor to feed her children, Mom was again like that child with an empty belly, a moon with no tide. She could not escape this loneliness and I barely knew her anymore.

I didn't see much of Mom then, or at least not awake. Damey began his career in sales and moved out. Hutch and I went to college. Mom had to face her demons alone spending many lonely nights while Dad was still running around the world of advertising and was chained to his job. We had all run out of ideas and energy to help her fill her voids so the best thing for her was to leave her alone and figure it out for herself. And she did.

Eight years later Mom sobered up. I had a mother again. We had become friends, something I desperately longed for, wasn't sure I would ever know and didn't even think it was possible after watching her self-destruct. We had found a spiritual connection now as adults and shared stories of romance, vision hopes and dreams as only a mother and daughter could. She had grown a softness in her sobriety, a compassion, a soulful understanding of the world around her. She developed an inquisitive spirit. The twinkle in her auburn eyes returned and I had come to not only know my Mom again but admired her new found strength to pull herself out of the trenches she had buried herself in for so long and let go of the side effects of a tumultuous childhood.

Then one day Mom decided to run away from home. Not in the literal sense where she packed a thermos, a toothbrush and emergency money stowed away in a pair of socks. She didn't traipse across the country looking for the meaning of life. It was the seventies and you were nothing if you hadn't a philosophy of life in which to draw from and which had no more significance than freeze-dried water. She didn't call home after seeing her picture on a milk carton with the inscription, "Have you Seen Me?" And she never remotely admitted to an even vague recollection of having had three pain-in-ass children who once deserted her and one husband who worked too much.

No, instead she napped in the early afternoon, having been exhausted no doubt from waking in the late morning. Mom loved to sleep. She was the only woman who slept through labor during the birth of her three children, Dad used to tell me. No one much complained as it was better to see her sleep then drink. So Mom rose three hours later every afternoon, shuffled herself to the kitchen in the old worn out Dearfoam slippers that comforted her in her drinking days to make her favorite snack...a half-cheese sandwich with thinly sliced tomato cut right above the core for its perfect roundness. She lipped each bite as if it were a gift from the "Sandwich God" then planted herself on the overstuffed couch to watch her favorite cartoon.

The Road Runner became her constant companion. That black bird with gray tuft on his head, legs spinning so fast they could polish stone. His nasally "beep-beep" resonated throughout the house everyday at three o'clock as he spent a half hour outwitting Wiley-D-Coyote who tried to catch him. I didn't mind one bit that my Mom, a grown woman found her peace and happiness after a good nap and a half-cheese sandwich watching a bird on crack-cocaine. At least she was alive and well and back to remembering who I was again. I loved my Mom now even more. In between naps and cartoons Mom and I would talk endlessly on the phone and would occasionally fly down to Atlanta to where I had just relocated for a teaching job after graduating college. Life was complete for us both and there was no better feeling than that.

I remember it like it was yesterday. A sultry day typical of a southern afternoon in August. My turn to mow the lawn and with each step a river of sweat poured off my brow and neck, the heat so fierce I could have easily hallucinated. Andrea my roommate yelled to me from the kitchen.

"You have a phone call." I mumbled a few nasty words under my breath as I approached the phone.

"There's been an accident. Your Mother." I was perturbed that Dad had pulled me off the lawnmower and broke the dripping sweat.

"This is not funny Dad. I'm hot and I'm crabby." Obviously it was a ploy to get me to the phone and I found no humor in it at all. But Dad's words fragmented as he collapsed at the other end. The nurses held him up and took the phone from him.

"Your mother was in a car accident. A young driver hit your mother head on. She died instantly," the nurse informed me in an authoritative voice. Mom, in her small blue Chevette didn't have a blazing chance against the inexperience of a young driver and an oversized Lincoln. My disbelief turned to horror as the phone now fell from my hands. I had to go home.

There was something strange about the quiet of my bedroom that afternoon. I packed for the unspeakable drive back to Ohio and tortured myself by pounding my fists against the bed frame. There was an eerie feeling surrounding me as I sat on the edge of the bed in a capsule of wonder.

"How could this be real? It wasn't real, I'm sure of it. It must be a nightmare, heat exhaustion, that's it. I am hallucinating. I knew I would it's so hot outside. And this doesn't happen to young people and it surely doesn't happen to my mom. She was only fifty-five years old." I choked on my own words.

The quivering of my body overshadowed the stale air outside. I shook my hands in a tireless repetition as if they would detach and somehow fall from my wrists and stave off the wrenching ache in my heart. I hummed absently with the songs of the winds outside my window, their magnificent voices rising and soaring as if to somehow lift me up and soften my mood. I then found myself stopped cold by a luminous peach glow upon my dresser mirror, an aura that lit the room to a candle's blaze. The copper and golden slivers of light reflecting off the mirror penetrated through the room and enveloped me as would a warm, soft fleece. How ominous and yet strange I thought as I stared for a minute, then two, then five yet feeling a comforting warmth all over my body. I thought my eyes certainly were playing tricks on me as I reached up to brush back my hair and feel my forehead as if to regain a sense of reality.

A warm current of energy surged through my spine as if a warm fleece blanket was thrown over my shoulders. My body had been trembling uncontrollably up to now. I was no longer experiencing the earthly anguish of physical pain. It seemed to have disappeared. And yet I still wondered, what had happened to the lights?

I mustered up the energy to walk back into the living room where Andrea and Alyssa were sitting on the couch wondering what to do.

"Who forgot to pay the electric bill?" I stammered, annoyed at the inconvenience.

"No one, it's been paid. And why do you look like you've just seen a ghost?" I hadn't realized the expression on my face was more of a startled one than an inquiring one.

"Then why did all the lights go out in my bedroom?"

"No lights went out here," Andrea reiterated. "And let me help you with those bags." Andrea, the friend who had handed me the phone only hours earlier couldn't help but take my arm and walk me back to my bedroom and cry.

"I don't know what to do for you, your mother was so young. Maybe I could help you pack."

"The lights went out in my bedroom. I swear. There was only the light of a candle. I stared at it for a long time. I was mesmerized by it and I felt warm as if nothing could harm me. Why would the lights dim like that? This is not what I need right now," I muttered through moistened, quivering lips.

"Sure they did, honey, sure they did." Andrea nodded her head and hugged me.

Hutch arrived shortly after to pick me up for the twelve hour drive home back to Cleveland and Dad. Neither of us knew what to do, what to say, what to think and how to cry. Silence, sobs, silence again, more sobs. Hutch, the youngest, the baby of the family, Hutch with the dumbo ears that grew to fit his head, the one who would hide behind Mom for protection from the tickling fingers of the two older siblings, was now holding me up as I bent over and vomited.

Hutch drove on without a word. I finally sat up and straightened my back against the front seat to regain some composure.

"The strangest thing happened tonight as I packed my bags. My lights went out in my bedroom. My bedroom was lit up like there was a candle reflecting off my dresser mirror for ten minutes. Ten whole minutes." I sobbed again. Hutch listened intently trying to understand what I was trying to say in between the words while trying to catch my breath.

"My lights went out and I sat on the bed and I felt really warm. It was soothing me, calming me down. It was the strangest feeling I ever had. My mind must have been playing tricks on me. It was like a candle light reflecting off my dresser mirror....I sat there for ten minutes and it felt so good like I could have melted," I repeated myself. How is that possible to feel that calm when Mom just died, violently only three hours ago?

Without hesitation, Hutch pulled over as if he was suddenly shocked back into reality, got off the highway and stopped the car. He then turned to me, his face as pale as oatmeal.

"What time did that happen?" he asked with a stunned look on his face.

"It was about 7:15, I don't know, seven something, just about an hour before you picked me up. I was trying to pack a bag but could only sit on the edge of my bed and stare at the mirror."

Hutch looked at me, then down at his feet as if he had just been knocked over the head by a brick.

"The same thing happened to me too. My lights in the condo went out at that very same time, 7:15. I didn't really know why either."

Hutch, my baby brother, now, my pillar of strength, took my hand and we both cried.

Mom had come to say goodbye. Maybe she was apologizing for all those years when she was drinking heavily and wasn't there for us. Maybe she came through now with a glowing presence, a light and a warm feeling to let us know she will never really be gone and wanted us to know that. We both then knew, that Mom was not leaving us without saying so.

I buried my mother over and over again that year. After the funeral, I found her journal she had been writing and had hidden in her dresser drawer. Each time I ran my fingers over the pages I pressed her words softly against my heart as if they could osmotize into my soul so I would understand what she had been feeling.

Her words took me into the undisclosed places I suspected she had been hiding in so many times during her life. I imagined myself, a starving child in an empty home without a father's love and a mother who tried so hard to keep her children alive. I felt Grandpa's evil ways as I read her stories and envisioned Grandpa slapping around Grandma when the liquor took over while all four children disappeared behind the couch. My heart would quiver at the thought of being given away to an orphanage with no family and no love. I knew she never wanted me to know what she had gone through. She was not going to intentionally abandon me like she had been just because she died. She had been afraid of so much and now left me her songs. I came to realize that my own soul had been seeded and full of forgiveness when I was denied my mother. Now, for a second time.

That was the day that changed my father's life. From then on, Dad pined away his days in bucket loads of photographs and bottles of Scotch. Sentiment washed over him choking out emotions he never knew he had. He was nothing without the woman who had given him her heart, a best friend, a home and children. For him the planet had stopped short and fell in to a bottomless pit, residing in a black hole that no one cared, nor knew about. The devil had gone too far, had chomped at the core of his existence, dismantling his reality from his soul.

Dad buckled himself down on Mom's bed every morning with his head between his knees and sobbed. Every moment turned into a year, every day, a lifetime. Mom would not be there for him to retire. She would never see her children marry. She would never know grandchildren. And she only knew peace for a few short years.

Dad grew impatient and delusional. He too, was young and had never been without his soulmate. He waited for Mom's return. He didn't eat. He didn't sleep. No one would tell him that his grief distorted his logic. Instead he milled about the house before sunrise every morning to see if she was coming home. Each sleepless night trickled into a fortnight. He tried calling her on the telephone and I had to gently hang up the receiver and hold him close while he wept when she didn't answer.

"She'll be back today," he'd mutter this to himself, over and over again. He thought if he said this enough it would come true, she would come home. Maybe that day. Maybe the next. His mind condescended into idle drops of despair. He would never be the same again.

....

Dad's body eventually wore down from the loss of Mom. He had given up and eventually succumbed to disease. He was now withering away from cancer. The diagnosis, multiple myloma. Prognosis dim. He was only sixty years old.

I tried hugging him but it was painful. His bones were like visible land mines protruding out. Skin dried and flaked onto his clothes and bedsheets. His hair grew white and became like a dead moss field that had no more growth. His face took on the color of weathered stone. His disposition told me that it was not nice to stare, or touch, for every last cell he had was dying. One eye focused while the other eye tried to escape to the side like he was looking into his ear for an answer. The morphine took his body hostage and he scratched uncontrollably around his face and chest, without purpose, while flailing his arms in the air trying to catch something. It was hard to watch him and remember what a handsome Irish lad he had been just a few years before, a bright hue that decorated his face in a whirlwind of expression. I tried to fill his loneliness with my presence and stories of the day.

Dad reached over to me and tried to be something of a host. He forced out a strained chuckle when his only grandson Gerard had made a snowman out of butter-scotch candies that someone had left him in a fruit basket. As if to make a sour moment sweet again.

"Look," Dad pointed upwards. "There's an angel on the ceiling. She's watching us, can you see her?" Dad touched my arm and chuckled softly. I hadn't seen a smile for a long time and it was enough to sustain me through the moments to come. I looked towards the direction of his eyes and saw nothing.

"The angel is sitting there. She is right there above the mirror. Look up, you can't see her? You must tell her to come down." I glared back at my father with a stubborn look thinking he had been teasing me and thought how he once stood so tall in his war-torn glory and now he was so diminished. My heart ached for him.

Aunt Sally, Mom's only sister, sat at the bedside with me as she watched Dad, her only brother-in-law, as he lay breathing. Sally was Mom's only sister but seemed to take a liking to the role of mother to the brothers and I. She was always there when Mom couldn't be and was especially present now.

"Spend your life wisely," she would encourage us. "It could be gone in an instant." We hadn't counted on life being so short and fragile. "You must stay together now, you and the boys." Sally knew this was not the time to isolate one another and instead rally for the strength we would need in days to come.

Sally wanted to be Mother Theresa or at least the likes of her. She would've followed the Pope into a medieval battle if it meant she could be recognized by God for something, anything. God would save her for a particular day, pick her up by his magical fingers and stow her away in a secret pocket in His robes of glint and glitter, only to take her out when he needed her. He would then set her on top of the world waving her wand of gold, feeding the hungry and scolding the wicked, while God took a break to whittle out the rest of creation. But instead she was thrown into the lion's den and had to face life and death in practically the same moment along with the rest of us.

Hutch and Damey could never view Dad's cancer, or life for that matter, from the same page. They were years apart and had differences in measuring a person's worth. At times I couldn't understand how they flowed from the same blood line. In spite of their different views of life, I, the sister in between wanted to be connected with them both, so I had someone to count on, somewhere to fall.

"It doesn't mean anything." Dad had mumbled these words as if his lips could form the curve of a word that meant so little to us. "The fighting. You kids need to get along. It doesn't mean anything in the end." He didn't exactly say that. He wanted us all to shut up and pay attention to him, is what he wanted. But I preferred to think that his wisdom in death was far greater than our bickering in life. "Nothing matters in the end. You can't take it with you when you go." How cliché, I thought. But we, Hutch, Damey, and I, were still here for the long road and figured we'd deserve to bellyache about it all the way to the end, anyway.

When Aunt Sally became sick with a pancreatic cancer she was only fifty-seven. She lived five years after a lung was removed from lung cancer but grew shallow and sunken deteriorating this time at a fast pace. Sally didn't want to budge. She wanted to go nowhere so held onto her life as if she were grabbing a tethering line. We hadn't expected something like this so quickly after Dad's diagnosis and we were confused as to why there was hardly a commercial in between the screen play.

Sally held on for Dad to go first. I'd like to think that everyone up there in Heaven was gathering up the welcome committee for them both. But like a courageous holocaust victim, Sally eventually starved to death refusing all treatment, choosing to die rather than be constantly vomiting from the chemotherapy. If only God had seen her clenching her fists in a fit of rage, aghast that he would take her next, if only He had recognized her overflowing conviction to live and protect us from the devil's bite, He certainly would have dismissed her fate as a cruel joke and changed her destiny right then and there. But He didn't, and she ended up on the quarter acre of land checkered with everyone else with the same last name.

Uncle Bobby was the youngest of the siblings. He died before anyone knew that time could age us and three weeks before I was born. He had barely become of age when Non-Hodgkins lymphoma took over his young life. Just as I was born, Bobby was buried. I never met him but often thought of how he began the cycle of bad luck. It was as if God planned to erase our blood line from the planet for no known reason. Maybe God needed the space for the Japanese people, who seemed by now to be taking up all the space on the other side of the globe.

Next was Uncle Eddy. Uncle Eddy was unaware of the impact he had on us. He never sobered up long enough to find out. But we loved his visits anyway. Eddy was a happy drunk. He would drink to be happy and be happy to drink. He was a funny drunk, too, if you could stand his eyes rolling around in his head like marbles in a slushie.

"Okay, Shorty," he'd begin. He called everyone "Shorty," including Damey who by now had grown to six feet tall. His tongue swelled from the hops and bubbles and by the afternoon his words sounded more like Elmer Fudd than the naval petty officer he aspired to be.

"Pwease, pwease, Mr. Wabbit," he would say almost losing his breath laughing. "Goodness, gwacious, I don't wook one itty bit wike a wabbit." An emphysemic roar followed a belch paling the power of a crack of lightning. It didn't help that the two packs of cigarettes he inhaled not only charred the deep caverns of his lungs, but deepened his voice to a deafening roar when he chortled. I think he liked to hear himself talk. Then he'd pull me close.

"Well, Shorty, how's about a big ole' smack-a-roonie for your ole' Uncle Ed?" Then he'd lock his lips onto mine making a squeaking noise as if somehow it was supposed to be a game.

"Cut it out, Unc. You smell like feet." I'd push him away. I did love the attention he mustered up for me, his only and apparently favorite niece, but was still confused as to why he always needed to touch me in places my father never would.

Uncle Eddy was not a large man. He was also a lonely guy who lived with his mother past puberty, after adolescence and into adulthood, at which time he decided to join the Navy.

Eddy's tour brought him to London on the naval ships from San Francisco. This is where he met and married his wife Jackie, an actress and dancer in the local theatres. He found solace in a woman who finally loved him in spite of his slow death from alcohol. I was never to meet Aunt Jackie but we spoke often on the "telly."

"Putti, Putti," in her British accent. "Do come for a visit. Your uncle would love it so." She spoke with pure admiration for her new husband's family even though we would never set eyes on one another. But I knew Eddy would have me visit because he loved me very much. Perhaps too much. He made me feel as if I was the only girl in the world who owned his heart, the most beautiful creature on God's green planet.

Nevertheless, Aunt Jackie loved him fiercely and without regret. She was what he needed to become a better man. So Eddy finally sobered up, got himself a civilian job in London where they resided, had small bits as an extra in the movies, small bits of character acting in the theaters in town, a bungalow in Middlesex, London and a shot at a comfortable life.

A few short months into his sobriety, Uncle Eddy fell off a scaffolding that held his painter's ladder while trimming the bungalow in the suburbs. His heart had weakened and exploded from the damage he had already caused by the drink and there he fell to his final place of rest. Another young life robbed of old age and another piece of my heart broken. He was only forty-eight years old.

Here now Dad was different. He wanted the life he had been given on this earth with the woman he had loved since a boy. If she wasn't to be with him, he would go to her.

I was trying not to ask him about the pain, or what it was like to die. Maybe we could visit the Bahamian shores next year, I told him. I knew my verbal cleverness couldn't save these moments and I watched him fade into oblivion while his mouth circulated without words. He reached towards my chair and dropped his arm alongside the bed as if there wasn't an ounce of strength left. He then managed to speak in garbled and yet surprisingly coherent words.

"I love you my spicy little redhead.... And I love that baby, too," his grandson growing inside of me. There it was, those words. I had never heard those words as harshly as I was now. You can't possibly love me I thought, if you die. I wanted him to explain to me why God keeps taking away everyone I love. What have we done to offend Him? Was there really a God? Or was He just a story to keep us from killing each other? Dad then stroked my face, in a weakened and absent way. I don't know if he was paying attention or just saying "goodbye."

"Could you do something for me Dad?" I asked while trying to regulate my breathing to disguise the inevitable sobs. "Could you come back to me and pinch against my left cheek?"

Aunt Sally had made that promise to me. Long before her death. She promised to brush against my left cheek, be it with the wind, or the sun, or a moon beam, just so I would know she was there. It was a long shot but a comforting thought nonetheless.

"Would you come to me like your angel has?" I pressed on. I thought to myself as I stared at him that he had always promised me he would let nothing hurt me. And yet here he was, ripping my hearts to shreds.

I had just been married and was ready to give birth to my first child. I was sure a grandchild would give Dad reason to fight. Instead we spoke little of the child growing inside of me. I forced a smile to disguise my dismay of the timing of life's surprises. Trying to drown out the bitterness blazing in my heart, instead I commented on how blessed I really was to have my father witness his growing grandchild when Mom couldn't be there. I wanted him to hold on a short time longer without letting him think his battle was fought. But we only spoke of laundry and mail.

Dad drew his last breath three days before my son was born. Time had frozen. I was ecstatic at a beginning while suffering an end. I was suspended into a space and time where I could be one with them both, another dimension with no pain, only vision. If only Mom were here to tell me her story, again and again of exchanging her brother for me. "One goes up, the other comes down," she'd say just to make light of birth and death and heaven and earth simultaneously. So when I saw my baby emerge from the womb, he possessed the same fuzzy, gray hair and distressed beaten red Irish face. Just like Dad. He bellowed out the anguish of his first breath when Dad had just taken his last. I knew this was his way of saying goodbye and Mom's strange and yet unique way of again sending me her songs.

That was the end of a decade. Not a one lasted long enough to retire. No one would walk Damey, Hutch or I down the aisle, meet their grandchildren, be fitted for dentures or enjoy the early bird special for seniors at the Red Robin. The family plot was filled. We buried Dad with all the others on the same quarter acre of land bought years before so everyone could stay together through eternity just as planned.

The ivy suffocated the headstones like craggy claws of a witch. Someone had already been to the property and brushed back the dirt collected over Grandpa's gravestone inscription. "Edwin, Father to Four, when he wasn't crocked or in the Pokey." At least that's what it should have said. Next to him was grandma Arla, "Mother of Children She Could Barely Feed." Even Grandma May's headstone, the one who had never missed a meal stood upright and towered over the other measly sandstones to let us know she was still in charge. Mom, Dad, Uncle Eddy, Uncle Bobby, Aunt Sally, together like a bunch of rare Japanese grapes, layers peeled away and yet growing from the same eternal vine.

The trees were smaller this time. The branches reached out in a skeleton's grip, and were the only vertical tenants in the cemetery claiming this territory as theirs. They seemed to be chanting a mantra along with the winds, as if to say, "Here we are, together again, with no particular place to go."

Uncle Riso was the only one living amongst us now. He was brother to Dad and not going anywhere. He would be sure to never part this mortal life so young, at least not unless the earth imploded or the west side of Cleveland and suddenly careened into outer space on its own accord. Even then, Uncle Riso would hold on for dear life.

No, Uncle Riso had other plans. He had been living with Dad up until the very end. His job was to sleep at odd hours of the day, get up at midnight and paint portraits of local politicians and celebrities. He often complained of jet-lag although he never much travelled past the Food Mart and that was only to catch a glance of his sculpted ass in the reflection.

But mostly, Uncle Riso was there to make sure Dad didn't fall out of bed. Dad had already done this before. The morphine not only made him see angels pirouetting from the ceiling like children cloaked in q-tips but made him groggy enough to roll, like a plump, wrinkled raisin, off the edge of the bed. Dad managed a snort when he spoke of this, which in his weakened state substituted for a session of hysteria as he described his roller coaster ride to the floor. Then he rubbed his front teeth with his forefinger, as a way of regrouping his thoughts and getting back to business, grimacing in pain and showing me how miserable he really was. Maybe I should've pushed him out of bed more often, just to lift his spirits.

Dad's house had been turned upside down after Mom was gone. He didn't recognize items strewn across the floor with grease and scum, or the piles of dirty laundry, or old crusty food on the counters and sink. He let the Reader's Digest pyramid themselves until the ceiling fan knocked them off one at a time. If lucky, he remembered to flush the toilet. Linens lay on the floor, soiled and musty. On counter tops lay cans of creamy soups half-opened while old toast still stuck in the toaster, taking on the color of green eyeshadow in a burlesque show. Mounds of collection notices and medical forms written in microscopic mumbo-jumbo went unnoticed under weeks of rolled up newspaper.

Damey was the first to arrive at the house. He not only brought with him a hand-strewn bag with braided straps but a notion that "He with the most toys, wins." It was a contest for him. Here was my heart, plummeting into depths in a way that normal lose won't take you and there's Damey, less the capacity to feel, toting an arsenal of luggage and a garage sale mentality.

Damey cruised the living room looking for anything of value, anything of substance, simply put, everything he could pick up. He loaded up with candlesticks and silver platters running ahead of the rest of us who had arrived and were content to stand motionless and wonder how it was one goes about choosing family heirlooms. Glass-blown pitchers, wooden statues with narrow torsos and pointed noses, pieces of fragile fertility that made no sense to anyone, Damey shoveled into his bags like the house was about to catch fire and he'd better be quick about it. I imagine Damey wanted to move on quicker then Hutch and I and being the oldest brother had the capacity to accept all this more than us.

Damey and Hutch were oddly different. Hutch would've much preferred one keepsake if only he could flee and end this chain of unfortunate events. Uncle Riso watched over the division of things to make sure that each of us were satisfied.

Hutch hadn't much cared for possessions as much as he cared for words. Objects and money to him were just in the way of a good conversation. Hutch had an interesting way to view the world. When he spoke of compassion for the poor or his travels through Australia he filled my head with dreams of grandeur. I admired Hutch's willingness to forgo nice things and replace them instead with an curious mind. Hutch learned long before any of us that life had come to us as a gift from God, and all creatures shared the same potential for compassion mixed with the right ingredients to survive and love. He could have walked out right then and there and never said a word.

Damey, however, fell from quite a different tree. I had admired Damey as a little girl. I thought his piercing blue eyes held an ocean full of ideas. He was a spittin image of a Greek god with a hard-on and was quite appealing to the eye. Even the girls, before they had boobs began trailing Damey, sure to betroth him before adolescence. I thought he not only moved mountains but hung the moon just for me, on a hanger and a lug nut so it could swing out of the clouds over my bedroom window when the sun went down.

I wanted him to reach up and taste the colors of the moonlight for me and touch the drops of light like they were jewels dotting our clothing. He could poke a hole in a darkened sky with his magical fingers for me to see clear to the other side of the galaxy or dance to the raindrops in a storm. I wanted to be at the core of his existence and glare at his beauty as he zigzagged in and out of my young life as an older brother would. Even I wanted to marry Damey, my own flesh and blood unaware that the probability was pretty great that our children would have iridescent blue eyes, on each of their three heads.

But now I felt sorry for him, assigning himself to be king of the siblings a right he had inherited through birth. I wondered if there ever was a sensitive boy, a magical lad beneath my big brother's skin. He succumbed to the fate of the family and wanted to move on without incident. And in a hurry. By now, Hutch was long gone.

My brain felt about a quart short of a gallon after watching the drama unfold. I had been carrying a load of my own what with the seven pound baby I had just given birth to only days before. I thought of the untimely luck of bringing a baby into a family divided, a whole world broken into pieces. I wanted to stick my infant son back through my keyhole, push him into my pouch for safe-keeping and dial back to the year before when I hadn't been privy to such obvious life-altering changes. I didn't want my baby knowing that the world had flaws, that wars were started for nothing more than wealth and power. That people hide in our own country to destroy our way of life, our freedom and kill their own children along the way. I didn't want him to know that when the Bible talks about "inheriting the earth" it didn't mean acquiring furniture and lamps. Someone had missed the point. But mostly I just didn't want my family, my home and the way we had grown up in to end, the way it was ending.

The house was put up for sale. A year later I saw it boarded up on one side, caving in from rotted wood. I had imagined the ghosts of "time gone by" to be sitting around on the sofa where Mom had laid intoxicated for the better part of a day and where Dad had paced through the hallways waiting for images of the woman he loved to appear before his very eyes. I envisioned the stale smell of death burning my eyes and hardening my face into limestone as they shared secrets of the family's curse. The termites who had set up termite housing, termite malls and termite playgrounds even seemed to have moved on.

Someone had the foresight to place a bouquet of daisies at the front door. It must have been some time ago as they lay wilted and browned from the blazing summer sun. The house still smelled of mold and a morbid sweat.

....

Nine years passed and I looked over to my son who sat two seats away. He was playing a video game disguised inside a plastic motorcycle. He asked me how we were getting to Phoenix as the jet taxied slowly to its point of takeoff. I answered sarcastically that we will be riding in that motorcycle if we could only fit. Not taking me seriously he replied, "No Mom, that's not what I meant. Which way are we going?" For a nine year old he is tuned into our adventures but not always interested in my remarks. By now he has figured the direction we are going is where the sun is coming up.

Hours into the flight my son watches out the window. He notices the mountains have grown upwards towards the heavens almost poking a hole into the belly of the airplane. He cocks his head slightly towards me in question and I could see that the sun has illuminated his ear. He smirks with disapproval when I suggest this to him but he also knows that our whole existence is based on the uncanny ability to love completely without complete understanding.

The peanuts he is eating have become bombs and the pretzels his forts. He has strategically placed them between his plastic soldiers and yet they are the same size to him as the bodies of water on the earth below. He chuckles at his own enormity compared to the little dots and dashes seen from high above in the airplane and comments on the quilted landscapes below. By now the cabin pressure has blocked my hearing and I politely nod although I have already tuned him out.

I think of my Father. I think of the gift he gave me in his death. It was by grand design that life created dignity and purpose of the highest magnitude, my child. I am not looking for him to be a year, a month or even a day older than right at this moment. Every precious moment I look at him I am wishing to freeze. Every one of his moves, every sound he makes, every thought he possesses I wish to encase into the banks of my soul never for a second to be lost or forgotten. He wisps into my life like a willow and an angel's sunlight trails behind.

It is because of my Father that his spirit spoke to me almost as concisely as if he were next to me, stroking my left cheek. He was my son's angel of life and watches over him now as Dad's angel watched over him.

I used to think when I was a child that all the rains came forth with intent on the day someone dies. The thunder celebrated their arrival in the heavens and the angels catered to their every whim through piercing drops of rain.

When Dad died there were no thunderous claps, no lightning extracting from the clouds to announce a loved one's passing. No, there was a blueness above the earth that electrified an endless horizon and a silvery hue that emitted the feel of cotton fleece. Dad had found my Mom again. Paradise was his. The child was mine.

Two Unlucky Days

A jet-stream is a meandering current of high speed wind that blows from a westerly direction. It can exceed two hundred and fifty miles per hour. A Gulf-stream is a luxury jet that flies high above the earth reaching speeds of five hundred miles an hour.

These luxurious modes of transportation are owned and operated by corporations to transport important people to golf outings disguised as mandatory meetings of the minds. They are owned and operated by celebrities to escape the fanfare of daily life or simply get somewhere without the fans or the fares. Thousands of dollars are spent in fuel alone and the caviar, lobster and imported wines and cheeses are served with bottles of brandy rarely sipped by us common people.

I, however, am the one who takes care of them. I am the one who dons a cummerbund, gold buttoned jacket with silver wings and caters to their every whim.

I am now in the airport hanger just before the sun rises and where the private jet has slept peacefully through the night untouched by the chilly air. My blouse has been soiled from the night before after landing in a small town in Arkansas and lugging off dirty dishes. The crystal I gently place into the bins are no doubt the finest, so ornate that one has to admire the craftsmanship yet the illogic of fragile pieces riding in a high-speed bullet thousands of feet in the air. I personally think the expensive dinnerware is too cumbersome for such a small work space but the passengers think differently.

The pilots are scrubbed to perfection. Their shirts are starched not a wrinkle to be found and their shoes polished so pristine that their smile reflects off them all the way back up to their face. And except for Jerome, who has a nasty habit of nervously picking his zits in flight, they are as stunning as Ken Dolls.

The crew, two pilots and I stow the arriving morning baggage. The psi on the fire extinguishers are checked, floatation devices counted, first aid is intact. The western omelets and homemade cranberry muffins I ordered last night arrive and are loaded into the specialized hot plates cooking slowly to armor the cabin with mouth-watering aromas. Doors close and we taxi to the runway to begin our flight to Atlanta to pick up our passengers.

I sit on the cushioned leather seat big enough for a circus elephant's hind ass and put my feet up to relax knowing full well this day of endless take-offs and landings around the country will be a long one.

The cabin is empty as of right now so I turn up the stereo full blast and even the roar of the jet engines couldn't block out Whitney Houston's voice as I sing along with her. I watch out the enormous windows at the landscape below, buildings getting smaller and smaller like pieces on a monopoly board, roadways like shoelaces running circles around the lakes and valleys. We ascend into the clouds that today are like cotton balls peppering the skies. Spears of sunlight poke through and I bathe in the hypnotic drone of the engines and the beauty of flight. I make the sign of the cross, Father, Son and Holy Ghost and say a quick prayer that we stay safe all day as it is a common notion that if you are going to die, you most certainly will on an airplane.

After several minutes transfixed on the heavens, I rise and begin the morning's routine. Everything but me is ready for a perfect service for my executive big boys. I remove my jeans and soiled shirt and begin to change into my newly starched blouse and very expensive navy blue uniform I had brought on board for the day's work.

As luck would have it, between the parking lot and the aircraft hanger, and somewhere between boarding the plane, cleaning and polishing the silver, I find my skirt has slipped off its hanger and lay somewhere in the Cleveland snow.

After a few choice words that tumbled from my lips, the next thought was, "Oh shit....how am I going get out of this one?" My gut is turning cartwheels as I envision the next fifteen hours serving the most successful executives in America with a jacket, a cummerbund and underwear.

I frantically run to the cockpit and beg the pilots to save my sorry self and help me find something to wear. Not happy about it they radio ahead to the Atlanta flight based operations to have a car waiting for me upon landing. They were sure not to spare me at the humiliating chuckles as they rolled their eyes in disbelief at one's ability to lose their own clothes. Even Jerome stopped his zit-picking for a moment and now I became the brunt of the day's jokes.

Just over an hour the Gulf-stream lands on the private airstrip. Off the runway was a battered yellow Jaguar that looked more like a banana with wheels waiting just for me. I exit the aircraft and jog to my tax and not wanting to complicate my life further, I politely asked the driver to please take me to the nearest clothing store and "Don't ask." With two hours before my passengers' arrival, I was hopeful that I would soon find a skirt resembling a navy blue uniform and none would be the wiser.

A few miles from the airport, there it was—A Goodwill Store! Oh my God...am I going to be wearing a toaster? A lampshade with yellowing streaks down the side? A checkered vinyl tablecloth? Having never set foot in a Goodwill Store I imagined the worst. But there they were in front of my own eyes—racks of clothing with fabulous linens, chiffon blouses and polyester pants from the 1980's. The foam headless dummies displayed leisure suits the color of green eye shadow from a burlesque show, others wore the color of mud. There were woolen jackets smelling like Grandma's attic and shirts and wraps with polka-dots and shimmering squares. But I knew I had no choice.

And there it was, like a diamond in the rough a blue skirt, no frills, no fringe, no glitter or smell. Exactly what I needed to save my sorry irresponsible flight attendant self.

The elastic band around the waist had been stretched to infinity but I knew I could string it up in places to keep it from sliding down to my ankles. It was a deep blue at one time, just the color I needed but now was faded with age in particular spots. But I knew if I moved quickly and twirled like a flamingo dancer as I served my passengers, it would appear as if the sun was just reflecting off it at that moment and no one would notice. So I bought the skirt for $3.00 and returned to the airport. Problem solved.

Twenty minutes later, my passengers arrived and boarded the Gulf-stream. Like every other normal flight, I greeted them at the door.

"Good Morning, gentlemen. May I take your coat? Be sure to put your seat belt on and if you don't know how to do that you shouldn't have left home in the first place. A cup of coffee?"

Thank God they were used to my quirky humor and chipper morning greets which certainly helped in distracting them from even noticing that I was dressed in various shades of blue.

Many of the corporate heads were on board today. They loved the relaxing atmosphere and privacy during long flights as they traversed the country checking production, inventing new products and counting the money.

I loved my job. It suited my free spirit well and I loved being with these people. Mr. Hartman keeping me abreast of all his grandkids and showed off new family photos. Mr. Goodman kept telling jokes that I never got but was forced a giggle anyway because he wanted so badly to be the center of attention. And Mr. Pendelmoker who I especially loved although I could never pronounce his name without a shit-eating grin, climbed aboard demanding I say his name so he could chuckle at my mispronunciation, gave me a hug and took his seat. Yes today was going to end up being a good day. Until Mr. Stanley arrived.

Mr. Stanley sat in the front seat facing backwards so he could turn and peer into the cockpit from time to time. Dennis Stanley was the corporate henchman and overseer of all things gone wrong. The only person in a company of thousands of employees, the one man, the one and only creature who made me nervous and didn't like me one bit. But I got used to Mr. Stanley milling about the cabin, checking equipment and liquor supplies to see if everything was in its proper working order.

Mr. Stanley never smiled. He never talked to me; he never told a joke and never had a pleasant conversation with anyone. But there he was flying the country to find things gone wrong. I don't even know what his job was because I was too afraid to ask. Not to mention, Mr. Stanley was a spitting image of my father who just passed away the year before with his Irish pout, his curly white hair and hardened Irish face and an empty glaze coming through his bifocals that could turn me to stone.

Yes, he looked just like my Dad when Dad was in a very bad mood.

Hours into the flight I begin the dinner service. Filet mignon, cheese platter, lobster and honey carrots French and Italian wines. The china plates with gold rims shimmered with each plate served as we flew into the setting sun west over Nebraska.

I finished the meal service with the finesse of a dove in spite of the bumps and jolts from the air pockets outside. I seemed to glide up and down the aisle with the grace and ease now that I had my new skirt tied around my waist with a string so not to fall down to my knees....a wonderful cross country flight indeed. I jotted down special drink orders on the decorative cocktail napkins although I could easily remember each of their preferences....dry martini with three olives for Mr. Rowlings, a chilly chardonnay for Mr. Smythe, a bloody Mary with a stick of dynamite, oops I mean celery for Mr. Stanley. I pulled out the pen that was always nestled in my tight curls behind my ear and wrote the special requests as they ordered. Everything ran as smooth as melted butter over a corn on the cob. Unless, of course, I was near Mr. Stanley.

After dinner and drinks Mr. Stanley ordered a cup of coffee. His eyes set sternly on my forehead which tilted downwards towards his serving tray as I poured from the china coffee pot. I was sure his speculative gaze was trying psychically to tell me that my skirt was a fake, a string was holding it up and the faded spots were not from the shadows of the clouds one bit. No he was indeed telling me that he was paying me too much money for this sort of unprofessional nonsense, a uniform that didn't quite match up. I tried to block out the invisible daggers he seemed to be sending my way and concentrated on the coffee service yet trying not to bend my head too far forward so to avoid his searing look.

The next thing I knew, something dislodged from my head. The pen I had been slipping in and out of my curls, any other time secured and only partially exposed, managed to zip straight down like a spearhead first poking Mr. Stanley's ear before landing into his coffee cup.

I froze. Mr. Stanley jolted out of his seat and mumbled in disgust, wiping his pants with one hand and clutching his spoon in another as if to make mince meat out of me. Still holding the china pot and seeping in morbid embarrassment I stood stiff like a cadaver, eye to eye with the one man who looks for things gone wrong. I let Mr. Stanley wait a bit before regaining my composure and still holding the coffee pot and now decaffeinated pen, walked back to the galley as if I had just peed my pants.

The service was now officially over. I did my best to sweep through the cabin, strangely avoiding the front seat facing backwards and prepared for landing. We buckled our seat belts as the plane descended into Orange County, California, seven thousand feet, wheels down, four thousand feet, smooth landing, and brakes on, six lights, everything on schedule. I sat in the back staring into the cockpit as I had done a hundred times before only this time too afraid to look at Mr. Stanley who was conveniently seated backwards glaring back at me the entire time.

We taxied to our stopping point. I rose to hand out coats and briefcases, Mr. Stanley scrunching his eyes at me to remind me again as he had all week that I had shockingly left his overcoat in Memphis last week and proceeded through the cabin with the items from the back storage. I waited for the cabin to depressurize while the engines shut down. I approached the front exit door, head high and pushed upwards on the red handle to disengage the stairs. I purposely stood closer to the door than I normally would to hide myself behind the bulkhead as much as possible and save myself from Mr. Stanley awaiting my next blunder.

The door opened, slowly, stairs screeching upwards then out with the usual deafening sound like metal being ripped apart in slow motion. I peeked back at the passengers as I always did with the usual farewell, have a nice stay smile then felt the tug of the doors powerful talons. Turning again to face the door I was calcified to stone. Here my skirt, my long, lucky blue skirt, the skirt that sauntered and danced its way through the flight like a trapeze artist, the skirt that gave me the power to glide like an angel on ice, was now caught on the handle of the door and pulling me out.

My farewell smile turned to horror. The co-pilot seated in the cockpit only a few feet from me, disgusted by one's series of unfortunate events, yelled for me to jump back and grabbed my arm. Just as I was practically hoping the door would pull me full out throwing me on the tarmac so I could just blackout and be done with it, I ripped the skirt off the handle in the nick of time and was left with undergarments and bodily parts unveiled for Mr. Stanley to see.

We flew home that night without passengers, only an empty cabin filled with humiliation and disgust. Never could imagine the next day would be any better.

The eleven o'clock call came in that night from the scheduling office when I arrived home. Wasn't unusual to get a call for a flight just hours before a departure. I would have gone anywhere at any time on our Gulfstream, as the excitement of the travel and people trumped the agony of early wake up calls. Nor could I resist the obnoxious humor of Miranda at the other end of the phone.

"Get your ass out of bed and see the world." Even in the deepest of slumber, Miranda managed a chuckle out of me.

In my haze between sleep and awake, Miranda spoke from the other end of the phone.

"You are taking the President of Sylvania tomorrow morning. You depart at seven a.m. and pick him up at Dulles Airport in Washington D.C."

Okay I thought. The President of a light bulb company. Guess he can afford a luxury jet. Hell. I thought. He has the money. Everyone in the world buys light bulbs don't they?

"Oh, and don't show him your undergarments this time," Miranda laughed out loud.

After six hours of blissful sleep I awake to dress for the next trip and drive my usual route to the airport. The aircraft was already awake by the maintenance guys who probably hadn't even slept yet after putting the plane to bed the night before.

"Morning, guys." It was always nice to see them as they coddled their baby, the airplane, as if it were their only child.

"And morning to you Patti. Did you remember your clothes this time?" Geez news had traveled fast.

"No, this time I thought I would go naked. That way nothing can get caught on the handle and try to off me this time." We all laughed as if it was a normal thing for me to screw things up.

Like always, I go through my routine of checking equipment and stowing the morning's breakfast into their hot plates as the coffee is brewing. My mind starts wandering. Hmm I'm thinking. I wonder if Mr. President of Sylvania light bulbs knew Thomas Edison. God I'm funny. As I am going through thoughts of what one who makes light bulbs would be like to travel with, several government vehicles pull up next to the airplane. Hmm, I'm thinking again. I didn't see their names on the passenger list.

Moments later the airplane is surrounded by men in dark suits. Two of them board the aircraft and start searching around for something. Both present their laminated badges and introduced themselves. "I am Agent McDonald and this is Agent Johnson, F.B.I." Wow, not only official guys but cute to boot, not to mention, Mr. President of Sylvania must be awfully important.

Meanwhile, outside the windows I see all the baggage that has arrived laid out on the tarmac. Several more men in dark suits surround the airplane, checking everything around it. Sniffing dogs show up and one by one, smell the luggage and various other parts of the plane. This, I'm thinking is quite exciting. Clearly, they are all looking for something however I haven't a clue what.

"Good Morning, Miss. We are securing the airplane for your passengers today and looking for any unusual packages, boxes, things of that sort." Jokingly I say, "Well, look no more. The bomb is in the garbage bin." Now, one knows that one never, ever puts the words bomb and airplane in the same sentence, but being that Agent McDonald and Agent Johnson did not take me seriously, I deduced Agent McDonald and Agent Johnson may have merely been the FBI-lings, or as I say, "Agents-in-Training" because I could have been taken away in handcuffs at that very moment, but I wasn't.

All was cleared and we were ready to ferry to Washington, D.C. to meet our very important passenger.

At 8,000 feet I strolled to the cockpit with coffee for the pilots and the usual morning chat. A beautiful morning it was and a smooth flight. I begin the conversation to the pilots about our especially important passenger. "Jesus, guys, this President of Sylvania light bulbs must think he's something, the cat's meow, so to speak. Having the F.B.I. Check everything? He must really be full of himself."

Both Captain Dave and Co-pilot Tim look at me with scrunched eyes in disbelief and ask, "What are you talking about?"

"All this protection for him? For God's sake, he only makes light bulbs....screw it in, light on, light off," a sarcastic chuckle. "How important does he think he is? We've never had someone this paranoid on board before."

"Where did you get that idea?" they ask.

"Well, Miranda told me our passenger was the President of Sylvania. Of course I was only half-awake when she told me but really, all this for him?"

"No, Dear," they almost speak in unison. "It's the President of Slovenia."

"Oh Crap. I need a vacation."

The Funny Side of Inner-City

I remember the first Christmas of the millennium. We collected batteries, wood, and distilled water for the year 2000, the beginning of the end. We found we weren't the pioneers we had hoped we would be. We didn't traipse through mountains of snow to see if our neighbors survived. We didn't cook our hunt over an open fire or blanket ourselves in wool. Nor did we put hot coals in our socks to keep us warm, or load our shotguns for the vandals sniffing around to steal our money or our young. We didn't really have to survive anything. How wonderful it would have been to be able to show each other how much we still needed one another. Perhaps we could have been reminded, like in the olden days, that it is people who make the world go round, not our possessions. A little suffering would have enlightened humanity and brought us back to what was really important—giving us reasons to grow in strength. And yet here we are years later, none the richer in human spirit.

It is our children we depend on to keep us humbled. It is the young who never grow old. Their lives have no immediate destinies, only present journeys. Their minds are golden treasure chests adorned with curiosity and fraught with illusion.

Children know that Santa has kissed them goodnight. They have seen ghosts dance eerily past their bedroom windows after the sun put her day to bed. They have even seen God Himself driving alongside them in his Buick Regal. Jewels frame their faces. They enrich our lives and are as content as their heart desires. They recognize their own talents without inflating their own egos, and eventually grow to acknowledge their place in this world.

Children never cease to humor me. It takes nothing to excite a child. Give them a blank piece of paper and they will ponder which side is front and which is back? Give them glitter and they have struck gold. Tell a little boy you love his blue shirt and he will wear that same blue shirt all week, stains and all. They will giggle uncontrollably over a fart as if they had never heard one before. They believe the tales they tell you and always know their perception of the world without shame or guilt, without fact or fear. One Easter, a student told me that Jesus never actually rose from the dead.

"No, Jesus woke up one morning," he told me, "on a street corner." He even watched him take a leak. That was his reality and who am I to challenge it? Tell a child you have a headache and they will draw a stick figure of me, the teacher, with curly blond circles surrounding my head, droopy looking eyes, and lips tightened into a hyphen, as a headache is hard to draw. And with eyes the size of platters and a half-hidden smile, they hand it to me with big black letters saying, "I love you teacher," on their version of a get-well card.

Children will also make me feel like a rock star. They applaud when I walk into the classroom as if art class was the best thing that ever happened to them, not to mention they love making loud noises of any kind. They will frantically wave to me at the end of the day from inside of Mom's car as if seeing me for the first time in a year, announcing, "Mommy, Mommy, that's my art teacher."

"You do know that we just spent the last six hours together, don't you? And only five minutes ago I was zipping up your jacket and hugging you goodbye, right?"

But you would never know by the way they show off teacher to Mommy. It's as if we were the biggest prize at the carnival.

So here it all begins. I have just buried most members of my family, the divorce is final, and I have accepted a teaching position. Excited as I am, I am also overwhelmed with my new role as single mother and new home owner. And now I am thrown into a new adventure, just my young son and I, and not at all ready for the Christmas holidays.

....

It seemed like a matter of only minutes that I had been in my new school, although in reality it had already been four days. I was approached by a teacher, Mrs. Someone, and didn't know who she was.

"Would you like to be a Secret Santa?"

"A what," I responded.

"A Secret Santa. You pick a name and someone picks your name and we exchange gifts to our secret person for seven days."

Oh dear. Not knowing if I should be polite or just plain honest, I declined. I mean, when would I have time to buy little trinkets for someone I don't even know? I have no time at this point to even eat, as I am moving into a new house, decorating a new house, raising my son, taking classes at night, and learning a new job. Maybe not the best time.

"Well, it's too late. Someone already picked your name."

"My name? Does anyone even know my name yet?"

One quarter pissed, half embarrassed, and another quarter trying to put on the smile of a team player, I reluctantly put my hand into the hat and pulled out a paper with the name, Ms. Andrea Cooper.

The following day, I find a pleasantly wrapped small box in my mailbox. I unwrap it as I walk to my classroom and find a coffee cup, surprisingly embossed in colorful words, "Teachers are Special." I'll put it with the collection of my other coffee cups that pretty much say the same thing—Moms are Special, Dads are Special, Dogs are Special, Bankruptcy is Special, Athletes Feet is Special, Divorce is Special. I guess everything is special when you drink coffee from a mug. Nonetheless, it was cute and I went about my day.

Next day, upon arriving at school, I find an even prettier box wrapped in glitter and bows. God, my Secret Santa is not only creative in her gifts, but in decorating them as well. Inside was a silver broach in the shape of a G-Clef note, the kind that music teachers all over the world have stored in their jewelry collection. Another cute little gift. "I better get going here and start buying stupid little trinkets for my Secret Santa, Ms. Andrea Cooper. Put that on my list of another million things to do list," I say to myself.

Third day, a small bound thesaurus wrapped in a bow. Maybe I could find a word in there to replace the words, "I don't really wanna buy stupid trinkets for a stranger." Surprisingly, the words weren't in my tiny new book so I decided I better get to K-Mart fast and start buying stupid little trinkets for someone I didn't know.

After school, I pick up my son from daycare, come home to paint the kitchen, shelve the pantry, cook a dinner, write a paper for my college class, unpack more boxes, drink a cup of coffee out of my "Teachers are Special" cup, and find the energy to go shopping at K-Mart for my Secret Santa. Probably a good thing as we needed things for the new house. Bed sheets, check that off the list. School supplies for kindergarten, Kleenex, crayons, glue sticks, new shoes, diet Pepsi, and cat food. Did I miss anything? I'm wondering. "No, I think that about covers it."

I return to work the next day to find another package in my mailbox and now remember what I forgot to buy the night before. Gifts for my Secret I-freaking-hate-her-now Santa my ass, Ms. Andrea Cooper. I think I'm going to give her a coffee mug that says, "I hate Secret Santas." I chuckle.

At work again the next day, I now wanted to pretend I didn't even have a mailbox, but there it was. Another gift. A paperback book of funny stories for the crapper. Starting to feel a little bit bad that Ms. Andrea Cooper had received nothing thus far, I rushed through my day and left school to run to K-Mart.

I need just five little stupid trinkets, wrapping paper, and pretty bows. Now concentrate. Oh, I need light bulbs too, oh, and tools to fix the kitchen sink. That picture frame would look really nice above the fireplace. And a few frozen dinners tonight, as there is no time to cook. I fill my cart, pay the bill, and return home. Do I remember to buy stupid little trinkets for a stranger? Of course not. But now I have a better idea.

I will take my cute little trinkets, books, and jewelry, place them into another box, wrap them in my wrapping paper, and place various little bows of my own on them. I will then give them to my Secret Santa, Ms. Andrea Cooper, for the remainder of the holiday exchange and none would be the wiser. Problem solved. I just may like this lady after all.

I walk my head a little lighter today at school, a bit more confident and a whole lot more relieved that my Santa, Ms. Andrea Cooper, will finally get her gifts. I am full of myself by now, having had an extra hour of sleep, a full meal the night before, and some extra play time with my son. God, I'm a genius. I should write a book on how one should be such a genius in skipping out on buying stupid trinkets for unknown people and still get the job done. Yes, those last few days were a relief. Not to mention, Ms. Andrea Cooper was getting a whole lot of really nice trinkets from a stranger, which of course was now me.

The last day of Secret Santa gift exchange was the Friday before holiday vacation. Ms. Cooper, Ms. Andrea Cooper, approaches me early that morning in the teacher's lounge.

"Good Morning. I have something for you."

Ms. Cooper hands me a beautifully wrapped large box covered in holiday glitter. "How incredibly thoughtful," I am thinking. Here a woman I have barely spoken to, giving me a Christmas gift? Because perhaps I am a new staff member? What a nice welcome.

"Must be my twinkling blue eyes," I chuckle to myself.

"Well thank you, Ms. Cooper. But might I ask why you are giving me a gift?"

"Yes, it's for you. I am your Secret Santa."

The words fall plum right out of my mouth without my permission and there they were.

"But you can't be. I'm yours."

And there it was. Poor Ms. Andrea Cooper, getting back everything she had been giving me. I hid in the ladies room the rest of the day and didn't sneak out until dismissal.

....

Karla

Karla, like a kid from a lot of Hispanic families, got off the plane from Puerto Rico in the dead of a Cleveland winter, weeks after school had already begun. Karla knew English better than most kids her age arriving in the States fresh off the plane, and far better than her mother, step-father, seven aunts, six uncles, and twenty-two cousins, oh hell, practically the whole village of Jalapeno pepper-ville. Yes, the large family flew to America to join the other members who had arrived before them. All but grandma, who was too stubborn to leave her homeland and begin a new life.

Karla was beautiful. Her long, silky black hair outlined her bronze complexion and the pout of her mouth. Her eyes lit up like fireflies against a backdrop of vanilla ice cream. If it weren't for Karla's hand-me-down jeans, pulled at the seams from wear and tear after big sister wore them out, or the blouse that was twice her size, I would have complimented her on her extraordinary sense of fashion. Her nails, however, showing signs of grace in the color and villain in the length, polished and pointed like daggers, would certainly keep her from picking up a pencil even if she wanted to.

On this particular day in January, when the winter winds danced their way around the school building like gigantic smoke rings, Karla and her mother walked into the entrance door from the unforgiving winds, roamed three flights of stairs, and entered the classroom to meet me. I fully expected them to stay home that day in their warm beds, but being that their furnace had not been working in their tiny rental on 4th Street, they decided to stay warm in school instead.

Karla, nervous in her new environment, sat next to mom, snuggling as close as possible without ending up on the other side of her. I offered them both a chocolate mint which both gladly accepted.

"If you recall our conversation, Mrs. Ortiz, we need to talk about Karla's work, or, lack of work in her other classroom."

Mrs. Ortiz knew full well that Karla hadn't adjusted well to her new surroundings. Karla would rather speak in her native tongue to the other Hispanic boys, show off her nails, and fling her hair back and forth in a provocative way rather than do any work. But now Karla stared down at her knees looking neither at mom nor myself.

"I'm concerned about Karla's transition to high school. She spends far too much time in the classroom, playing with the other students, writing notes, giggling and ignoring her work."

No response. Mrs. Ortiz, watching me speak, nodded her head and rolled her eyes, or at least the one good eye over to Karla as the glass eye had no choice but to look straight at me, as if to fully acknowledge our conversation.

"As you know, Mrs. Ortiz, Karla will not make the grades to enter high school if she is failing history and science. Here is a copy of her history test she took yesterday."

I presented a page with several questions that had no answers. Except for the name she had given herself written at the top of the page, "Queen La'Karla," and a cartoon-like doodling of a shape that could easily have been taken as a penis and hairy boobs, the rest of the paper was blank.

Karla, too embarrassed to look up from her knees at me, glanced at mom who glanced back at me with a tight-lipped smile. Again, no response.

Ice crystals were whipping at the window and the wind snapped as I wondered about what to say that I may get a response from.

"I was hoping, Mrs. Ortiz, we could discuss some possibilities. A vocational school where Karla could learn a trade." That's what I could say.

I knew this move from elementary school to the upper grades would be big for Karla. Leaving the comforts of teachers who had mastered the art of baby talk and stern glances. Leaving behind free breakfast and lunch, protective fences, security guards and metal detectors. Moving to a larger building with higher fences and bigger boys with bigger ideas. It was a lot for her to adjust to.

More nods and tight-lipped smiles, mom looking at Karla then me, then nodding to Karla again. Quiet minutes passed. No one spoke. I was beginning to think I had been having a one-way conversation with an inanimate object resembling a human being with pasty tights lips and eyes like glazed donuts staring at me. Both Karla and mom folded their hands into their laps and tapped their thumbs against each other as if to unleash the answers to all things unknown.

"Mrs. Ortiz, I thought perhaps Karla could become trained, oh, I don't know, perhaps in the medical field.

What, with those deadly nails, I mean beautiful hands, she could maybe become a dental hygienist." You know, just a thought to snap them out of submission.

Karla, who now had been sitting quietly for twenty minutes, said something in Spanish to mom. I knew then that mom did not speak English at all and only smiled and nodded shyly out of respect. Karla smiled as she spoke to mom, obviously loving the idea. Dental hygienist. There it was, the words that would wake them both from their coma. Mom's face, which had been devoid of human life form for the past twenty minutes, now lit up and filled the air like a love song, her words flowing like whipped cream. Dental Hygienist, both were amused.

Mom and Karla exchanged words I could not understand. They spoke so fast, I was sure neither of them could understand what each one was saying. I know I didn't. Mom saw a future for her daughter. Mom saw an education, the road out of poverty. Something other than drawing cartoons of boobs with hairy nipples and that pleased her to no end. Mom looked back at me and much to my amazement, opened her mouth wide with the breath of a boisterous, full-blown muted scream. And there it was. A huge black hole, rotten gums and only one tooth crossing over another tooth as if they were hanging on to each other for dear life. I decided that my idea was not a real smart one, but an idea nonetheless. Off they went.

....

Samantha

Samantha hadn't arrived to school one Monday morning. Samantha, one of my prized fourth graders never missed an art class. One day turned into two, then two turned into three days, then an entire week that

Samantha was absent. The following Monday her face appears at my desk earlier than usual.

"Where have you been child? It's not like you to miss art class."

"I was home sick. I had a fever and my body hurt all over."

"Well I'm glad you're feeling better."

"Yes, I was home sick all week with fleas."

"Don't you mean the flu?"

"Yeah, that's it."

....

Identical Twins

Rob and Bob, yes identical twins. Rob, the one born three minutes before Bob. Personally I couldn't tell them apart so I just called them the Ob's for short. Possibly Mom had so many other children she decided to rhyme their names to make it easier to remember. Thank God mom didn't have triplets.

Anyway, Rob, or Bob, told me he had been home sick too. Rob had strep throat in his eye. Then Bob told me he was home sick too because his liver hurt. Well anyway, "Bob and Rob, or Rob and Bob, glad you're back to school today." They are in jail now for assaulting each other over an argument about who was better looking.

....

Randy

Randy had not shown up to school for five days. Not that I much cared because Randy needed so much attention and sometimes exhausted me to no end. Randy showed up the next week and the look on his face was droopy and sad.

"Can I talk to you please?" he asked me.

"Of course, Randy. What's wrong with you today?"

"My grandmother died."

"Oh Randy, I am so sorry. Are you going to be okay?"

"I don't know. I am really sad."

"Okay Randy. If you ever need to talk, come see me after school. I know how hard it is losing a loved one."

Randy didn't come to school the next day again, or the next. Now I was concerned that he was severely depressed over losing grandma. He was young and probably never experienced a death before.

The third day, Randy approaches me with the most amazing smile. I was glad that Randy had most likely talked to someone about his pain and adopted a more positive approach. He ran to me and hugged me so tight I thought he would end up swallowing me.

"Randy, so glad you are doing better and are getting through this."

"You can't believe how happy I am," he says. "My grandmother came back to life."

"Oh okay," thinking maybe he is a bit run down and perhaps delusional too.

"Randy, I'm not sure how to say this, but when people die, they don't come back to life."

"Oh yes she did." Oh dear God, I'm thinking. Do I need an Advil? Maybe four this time?

"Randy, now maybe before, your grandmother was in a coma. Do you know what a coma is? It's like a really deep sleep, but the person is still alive."

"No, the whole family sat with her and watched her die last week."

"So let me get this straight, Randy. Your grandmother died, then came back to life? Do you need to talk to the school psychologist, you know just to help you make sense of this?"

"Yes, it was a miracle."

"Okay then, glad you are back at school."

Two days pass and Randy is gone again. Now I'm getting worried that Randy, who is a young and vulnerable boy, might need a little assistance for his grief.

Three more days pass and Randy rushes to me at the opening of the school Monday morning and hugs me while tears dripped slowly down to his chin.

"Randy, what's going on, are you okay?"

"Grandma died again, but this time she sat up in bed and threw her arms up into the air like she wanted to jump into Mom's lap before she laid back down. That was it. Then she died again."

"Okay Randy. Is she really dead this time?" trying not to sound sarcastic.

"Yes she is and she waited for all of us to be together so she could say goodbye. That's why she came back to life in the first place, because my uncle wasn't there yet. She wanted us all to be together first."

Now Randy hugged me so tight I thought he was gonna end up on the other side of me. Dear God, give me the whole bottle of Advil this time. Extra-strength please. Oh, and throw in a new job.

....

Shannon

"Time for lunch, kids. Put your art supplies back into your cubbyholes and let's have the quiet children line up first." Everyone talking and giggling runs to the door at the same time. "No, I said quiet ones first."

"We are quiet."

"You mean to tell me when you're talking, giggling, and jumping around the room like monkeys, you are quiet?"

"Yeah."

Oh boy. "Okay, make sure everyone has their lunch boxes," I remind them.

Shannon, the only one not running to the door, talking and giggling and hanging off the tables, is still seated and raises her hand.

"Yes, Shannon?"

"I forgot my lunchbox."

"Where is it?"

"It's in my classroom."

"Well we can walk down there and pick it up first. Is your teacher in there?"

"No, she's in the drinking room."

The Whistler

Today I cleaned out the pool for the last time this season. The chore should be easy this time with my new skimmer with the really long handle. This way I can reach to the far ends of the pool to scoop up the needles and debris that had fallen from the pine tree above, without completely submersing myself. Yes, the water's quite cold today and thanks to my new skimmer with the very long handle, I am glad I don't have to get fully wet.

I begin at the shallow end where most of the insects had either fallen in or purposely jumped in to commit "bug suicide." I don't know, maybe if I were a bug, I may tire easily of just crawling around in the grass all day with nothing else to do but bother people, and dive in to end it too.

With greatest of ease I move about the sides of the pool, skimmer net collecting the bugs then tossing them back out onto the grass. Then I hear a whistling sound.....zzzzwwwiiitt....zzzzwwwooo. Well that's strange I think. Who would be whistling at someone cleaning out a pool? It's probably the old man across the creek watching me for a thrill. He was 92 years old after all and no doubt as bored as the insects crawling around on the grass. Except the old man across the creek probably couldn't even see very good or he wouldn't be whistling at someone half-submerged in a pool with a an old torn t-shirt and hair flaming full out like a torch, that was so tangled, my blue heron could have laid eggs in it. But there it is again.....zzzwwwiiitt....zzzwwwooo as I continued to discard the insects back onto the grass.

I go about cleaning, saving five lightning bugs still struggling to swim. Gotta always save those lightning bugs in case I need them someday when the power goes out you know. And so many spiders. They must have been living miserable lives as their spider legs were outstretched as if they were trying to swim from one side of the pool to the other, before calling it a day. And there it was again. Zzzwwwiiitt.....zzzwwwooo I hear as I throw the drowned creatures to the side.

I now reach towards the far corners at the deep end of the pool outstretching my arms as far as they would go with my long-handled skimmer with its net to collect more debris and toss it to the side....zzzwwwiii....zzzwwwooo... Oh my God, who is whistling at me? I look over to find the old man and see nothing. Not even a deer or animal caught in the brush making any sound even remotely resembling a whistle. Is someone hiding behind a tree and going to jump me?

I finish the task and climb out of the pool, satisfied that it is ready to be covered for the winter. I climb the steps to exit out of the water, carrying my new skimmer with its very long handle. As I get out and pull up my new skimmer up, there it was again...zzzwwwiiitt.zzzzwwwoo.

The air had been escaping out the hole at the end of the handle each time I brought it to the surface to discard my treasures and whistling all the while. There was my whistler.

The New Mail Lady

Our neighborhood has a new mail carrier. Wasn't quite sure if she was a mail carrier cause when I watched her canvas the neighborhood she did not have on the mail carrier uniform, only blue shorts that touched her knees and an off green baggy t-shirt. Not the typical garb of a full-time federal employee.

After three days watching this new scruffy dressed lady, I finally asked her if she was delivering the mail or just stalking my house to see she was going to come back later to kill me. I thought I was being funny as she kept the pace of a moving bullet from house to house only to finally slow down to answer my question.

"Where is Larry? The mailman who has delivered our mail for ten years?" She stopped in her tracks and thought about it.

"He hath transferred the Fairview Branth." Not sure but I think she said he transferred to the Fairview Branch....

"Is he okay?"

"Heth fine, don't athk,"....So I didn't.

I really wouldn't have missed Larry one bit. I liked him because he was a constant figure at my mailbox, sometimes early, sometimes late. You never knew when Larry would really show up. But I didn't much mind as long as he did show up.

Although Larry was doing his job, or sometimes doing his job, I knew when Larry had moved on I was not gonna miss the cigarette butts strewn about the neighborhood like a trail of birdseed. Maybe he was going to try to find his way back to the mail truck. Larry talked to himself in between houses and probably lost all memory of who he was, where he was parked and what he was doing so the crushed butts would help him find his way back. And I sure wasn't gonna miss the mail I would get from dead people or the occasional income tax refund check swimming in a mud puddle that Larry never realized he dropped. Sometimes when Larry, after smoking like a sailor, spewing out bits of tobacco and answering himself to a series of questions, Larry would arrive back at my mailbox a second time since he never could really remember what he was doing when he was there the first time.

So although Larry was quite a nuisance and quite entertaining at the same time, I still got my mail. In fact I got everyone's mail. Electric bills, doctor notices, bank statements, invitations to the "Golden Club," birth announcements, Christmas cards and even one time a 35 mm camera. Thanks, Larry.

"So will you be delivering our mail?" I ask.

"Only for a thort time," she answered as her tongue gyrating from one side of her mouth to the other like it was trying to find a place to rest. Jesus, what kind of gum is she chewing, I thought.

Not to interrupt her rapid pace. I welcomed her to the neighborhood still watching her jaws swinging from side to side, tongue following every move, and practically falling out of her mouth. "Oh," I thought, "maybe she has rolling tongue disease?, whatever that was. Maybe a battery-operated tongue implant? Is she having a seizure?" I shouldn't even stare but couldn't help watching one cheek scrunching to push the tongue to the other cheek, as if it was perfectly normal to do this. Maybe she has a lisp, maybe just a nervous twitch. Too embarrassed to look any further, I instead locked my eyes onto hers, smiled and said, "Have a nice day, new mail lady." Next thing I know her mouth opened as wide as Texas to respond to my farewell, and there it was. A tiny silver round ball pierced into the side of her tongue.

"Thankths." And she moved on.

My Blue Heron

Nestling just feet above a silent creek a few of us call "The Hidden Bay" is a creature reminiscent of a prehistoric bird, the largest of the heron family, my Great Blue Heron.

I had never seen a bird like this until now, with wings spanning up to 70" wide and outgrowing the width of the creek. Its legs dangle behind her in flight as if they were barely attached to its torso. With her neck in an "S" formation she glides like a trapeze artist to and from her nest with only the peace and quiet of a magenta sunset trailing her.

She is beautiful with her white face and crown of blue-gray and black plumage covering the rest of its body. I watch her from the rocks on the sidelines. We have connected by chance and inadvertently developed a kinship. There like me, she exists alone in solitude, without a mate, and quite possibly having already sent off her young after only two months. And just like me, she seems content to be alive and comfortable in this moment as she stretches her balletic neck, while the magenta hues reflect off the lake and color our day as she stretches her wings to its fullest capacity just to feel the wind's magical forces.

Both of us marinade in the voices of our surroundings, the ducks. deer, and the migrating rainbow trout swimming by every October and March like holiday guests, before blanketing herself into its nest of pine needles, moss, reeds, dry grass and twigs while the darkness sets in.

The Blue Heron has adapted well in her home behind my house, preferring the inland trees and water. Plenty of fish, insects, voles, lizards and snakes provide her with a never ending feast.

The Blue Heron has not only captured my attention and affection, but my home as well. I rise in the evening to see her settle in for the evening then walk back to my kitchen door facing the creek. As she returns to her nest she has just dipped her wing my way as if to say "Goodnight." Goodnight to you too, my special friend.

Ed the Love Bird

Ed was his name. A love bird with a greenish tint flowing off his soft feathers. Ed was no longer singing acapella with his love bird wife Edna anymore, as she had flown out an open door one chilly afternoon and never came back. Ed never was sure if she purposely left him for another feathery creature or just saw an opportunity to be stupid enough to explore the outdoors. Edna surely had frozen to death after a few days as she was an indoor creature unfamiliar with the Cleveland winter cold.

I'm pretty sure Ed was depressed. His love bird persona needed a mate so he felt sure I would fit his void.

"Jwert-jwert," Ed would sing to me. Ed seemed to approve of everything I did. Particularly funny as I just divorced my husband who approved of nothing I did. So Ed and I were perfect for one another, each having lost our mates.

Ed pecked me on the cheek. He liked to do that often. I found it amusing because even the x-husband never bothered to peck me on the cheek. Or anything else for that matter so Ed was a nice change from the past five years. Like the surf on the sand, Ed was always there when I needed him and I wallowed in the feeling that something, someone, some whatever he was, needed me again.

Ed spring-loaded from my shoulder to my head and danced around as he had done a quadrillion times before. Ed's devotion to me was overflowing. Freed from his wired cage every day he explored each room and tracked my voice along the way until he found the launching pad on top of my head again. I finally had a dance partner. Or at least one I liked, each of us dancing to different songs in our heads.

"Where did ya go Ed?" I secretly hid from him behind a corner and watched. In hearing my voice, Ed would cock his walnut-sized birdie head from one side to the other like he was asking himself that same question. "Come find me, Eddie." I loved Ed. We seemed to understand each other. And since neither of us had a real life to speak of, which was evident in me having full-blown conversations with a bird, it worked for us. Ed didn't have a mother-in-law, didn't have a job, never missed a Visa payment and never missed a meal. Ed didn't really have any baggage at all as he quickly forgot his birdie babe that left him. Ed didn't have a care in the world and believe you me, I was reminded of that every time Ed flew over the stove and dropped a runny white one into my scrambled eggs. "Oh Ed, you are so silly."

Ed listened to me when I wanted to talk, which was often, when he wasn't flying into clear glass windows and knocking himself out cold, or doing a pirouette in my hair. No, we relished our time together as he danced around and around becoming pleasantly tangled in each blond curl.

One evening, after spitting birdseed all over the walls and floor, dropping a load on everything below him and "jwerting-jwerting" me crazy, Ed became particularly feisty. He launched himself onto my head and danced in twirls as if dancing to strange music in his head. Usually that would have been me dancing to strange music in my head since I had no life at all except talking to a bird, but no, not tonight. He must have been dancing to a waltz as he twirled around and around and around on my head as if he were hypnotized and didn't know how to stop, skinny love bird legs, the width of a paper clip, circling like he was on top of a music box.

Ed decided that was enough twirling then shot off into space finding something better to do, jetting himself into the open kitchen spaces. Or at least he tried to jet off into the open kitchen spaces. Ed made it about three inches before ricocheting back onto my head like a rubber band then fell off my head landing upside down abruptly right smack against my nose.

"JWERT-JWERT-JWERT"...Ed's screams got louder and louder as he tried to understand what just happened. Ed tried to take off again only to land upside down, for the second time, his eyes black as licorice and small as a period staring straight into mine. Panicking and revving his birdie engines, he tried to take off again only to be jerked back, finding himself upside down for the third time, his terrified eyes again meeting mine. Ed then pole-vaulted himself this time straight up, ironically landing back on top of my head.

Poor Ed. Tangled himself in his own nest which was the curly mop of my hair. Each time he had swirled around on my head, he was winding himself silly with each strand. His legs were now wrapped in my curls which by now were flaming full out like a torch as he dug his sharp, prickly birdie nails into my scalp to balance himself and hold on for dear life.

Ed was trapped. Neither of us knew what to do and I know that for sure because I asked him what we should do.

"Shit Ed...What are we gonna do?"

He didn't answer. All he could do was "jwert-jwert," now fully trapped on my head.

My only thought was to get the scissors and cut him loose. I pulled out the scissors and traveled to the bathroom mirror to see how I could do this and tried to cut him loose from my head. He continued his frantic two-step as I carefully placed the scissors where I wouldn't cut his toothpick legs in half, which may have helped the growing holes in my scalp but wouldn't help poor Ed to ever stand again. I then sliced a big knot out of my hair below his legs and there he was, free to fly away, although quite weighted down with his newly formed Eskimo boots.

The next morning, I woke up to check on Ed and make sure he didn't die of heat exhaustion overnight from my curly hair smothering his birdie legs. Ed was still spitting out birdie seeds and plopping white ones all over the cage, as he danced back and forth on his birdie throne waiting to be set free for his field trip around the house as he had done every day since Mrs. Love Bird left him. Ed, happy to see me and happy to be free flew about the house, "jwerting" himself with joy. Ed then heard my voice, found me in the kitchen and landed on my head and began his twirling ballet in my blond locks, over and over again circling like a clown on a unicycle. Let's just say Ed wasn't the brightest bulb on the tree.

Made in the USA
Charleston, SC
24 February 2014